THE TABERNACLE
SYLLABUS

Marilyn Hickey

The Tabernacle Syllabus
© Copyright 2010 by Marilyn Hickey Ministries
8081 E. Orchard Rd, Suite 135
Greenwood Village, CO 80111-2675

All Rights Reserved

ISBN 978-1-938696-08-4

All Scriptures are quoted from the *King James Version* of the Bible unless otherwise indicated.

Printed in the United States of America.

Table of Contents

Foreword

When Moses built the Tabernacle, it became the first time in the history of man that God humbled Himself to dwell among men. Think of it — the Almighty Creator of the universe and Master of all actually chose to come to earth and abide in the midst of sinful man!

For this tremendous occasion, God gave Moses detailed instructions on how to construct His home-to-be so it would precisely duplicate His home in heaven. Much of the books of Exodus, Leviticus, Numbers, and Deuteronomy are devoted to God's blueprint and the building of the Tabernacle, as well as the establishment of the priesthood and the ceremonies to be performed there.

The Tabernacle was more, however, than an earthly dwelling for God. Every minute detail—from color choice to the placement of each part—foretold the coming Messiah and His work of atonement. From the way the camp was situated around the Tabernacle to each piece of furniture, everything about the Tabernacle spoke of Jesus Christ.

The study of the Tabernacle is a thrilling look at our Lord Jesus Christ. As you closely examine the priesthood, the furnishings, and the sacrifices, you will see more about Who our Savior is and His love for us than you ever thought possible. As a teacher of the Bible, I love every bit of God's Word, but the portion on the Tabernacle is one of my favorite parts. Every time I study the Pentateuch, I receive new revelations of Jesus, allowing me to know Him more fully than before. Study this material with an open heart and an eager mind. I believe you, too, will find yourself more in love with Jesus than you have ever been when you discover Him through the Tabernacle.

His love and mine,

Marilyn

THE TABERNACLE
SYLLABUS

Section 1
THE TABERNACLE AND HOW IT RELATES TO YOU TODAY

Chapter 1

WHY STUDY THE TABERNACLE?

From Genesis to Revelation, the Bible is filled with symbols and illustrations pointing to some aspect of the Trinity. Moses reveals one such symbol in Exodus 25-40, when he recorded God's instructions to build the Tabernacle. On Mount Sinai, Moses received not only the Ten Commandments, but the blueprint to build a resting place for the presence of God.

The Tabernacle is a *type* and *shadow* of Jesus Christ, built after the pattern of the heavenly Tabernacle and symbolic of Jesus' death on the Cross, His atoning blood that was shed at Calvary, and His role as a mediator between God and man. It also foretold the day when God would send the Holy Spirit to indwell, or "tabernacle" with man. One of the most striking things about the Tabernacle was that it was shaped like a cross. The placement of the furniture, as well as the tribes that encamped around it, formed a cross, pointing all those who saw it to Jesus Christ the mediator (or meeting place) between God and man.

The study of the Tabernacle is a detailed one. Every time I study this subject, I become excited because I always receive fresh insight. There seems to be a continual unfolding of revelation on this topic.

The first time I heard about the Tabernacle, I thought, "Who wants to hear about a linen curtain and the construction of pieces of furniture?" But when I actually began to study the Tabernacle, I saw how the Scripture unfolded Christ to us and revealed our approach unto the Father.

There are many reasons to study the Tabernacle—for historical purposes, as well as for personal edification. However, two of the primary reasons Christians need to study it are because the Tabernacle gives a picture of Jesus in the Old Testament, and because it provides a current pattern for Christian life.

Romans 15:4 says, *For whatsoever things were written aforetime were written for our learning, that we through patience and comfort of the scriptures might have hope.* In other words, a study of the Tabernacle can give us hope because it illustrates God's plan of salvation was put into motion before the creation of the world and was not just something He thought of because nothing else seemed to work.

THE PATTERN

God instructed Moses to build the Tabernacle so He could dwell among His people. He said,

> For I have not dwelt in an house since the day that I brought up Israel unto this day; but I have gone from tent to tent, and from one tabernacle to another (I Chronicles 17:5).

The importance of the Tabernacle in the mind of God cannot be underestimated. He gave Moses the pattern to build it seven times, and there is more in the Bible about the Tabernacle than any other subject. There are forty chapters on the Tabernacle and only two on creation. Why? The Tabernacle would finally allow God's Spirit to dwell among men. Although God's Spirit had rested *upon* some people in the Old Testament, it was intermittent or sporadic at best and for a specific purpose. In Judges 14, for example, the Spirit of the Lord *came upon* Samson and empowered him to do the supernatural:

> Then went Samson down . . . and, behold, a young lion roared against him. And the Spirit of the LORD came mightily upon him, and he rent him as he would have rent a kid, and he had nothing in his hand . . . (Judges 14:5-6).

> And the Spirit of the LORD came upon him [Samson], and he went down to Ashkelon, and slew thirty men of them, and took their spoil . . . (Judges 14:19).

Throughout Judges 14 and until Samson's death in chapter 16, we see the Spirit of God coming *upon* him. Although God's presence empowered Samson to kill Israel's enemy, the Philistines, God wanted to permanently abide with Samson and all mankind. Hence, God told Moses, "Build me a place where I can dwell with you."

God's plan for the Tabernacle was that it would be His resting place where He could permanently abide with *all men*. His heart can be seen through His interaction with Moses in the building of the Tabernacle. God desired fellowship with a "body of believers" much like He has with the Body of Christ today. I believe God's plan was to inhabit the Tabernacle, which is symbolic of the indwelling of the Holy Spirit in New Testament believers.

Once established in Israel's midst, God manifested His presence in the form of a pillar of cloud by day and a pillar of fire by night, so He could teach them to follow His leading, as we are commanded to obey the prompting of the Holy Spirit. Exodus 40:33-38 is a beautiful illustration of this truth:

> *And he reared up the court round about the tabernacle and the altar, and set up the hanging of the court gate. So Moses finished the work. Then a cloud covered the tent of the congregation, and the glory of the LORD filled the tabernacle . . . And when the cloud was taken up from over the tabernacle, the children of Israel went onward in all their journeys: But if the cloud were not taken up, then they journeyed not till the day that it was taken up. For the cloud of the LORD was upon the tabernacle by day, and fire was on it by night, in the sight of all the house of Israel, throughout all their journeys.*

The Israelites literally feared God, but not in a reverent way; they thought He was unapproachable. In Exodus 20:19, they told Moses, *Speak thou with us, and we will hear: but let not God speak with us, lest we die.*

Unlike Old Testament believers who dropped dead because they offered "strange fire" to the Lord, or accidentally touched the ark, we can . . . *come boldly unto the throne of grace, that we may obtain mercy, and find grace to help in time of need* (Hebrews 4:16).

THE PIECES OF FURNITURE

Everything about the Tabernacle was holy, including the furniture, which was an exact replica of the furniture found in the heavenly tabernacle. Had Moses deviated from the pattern God had given him for the Tabernacle, God's presence could not have abided there. God is holy and will only abide in holy vessels. The Body of Christ has been made holy by the shed blood of Jesus Christ.

When God told Moses to build the Tabernacle, He said,

> *And let them* [the children of Israel] *make me a sanctuary; that I may dwell among them. According to all that I shew thee, after the pattern of the tabernacle, and the pattern of all the instruments thereof, even so shall make it. . . .*

*And look that thou make them after their pattern, which
was shewed thee in the mount (Exodus 25:8-9, 40).*

In giving Moses the pattern for the construction of this holy place,
God did not intend for Moses to build it by himself. As Jethro, Moses'
father-in-law, had instructed him to appoint men to help him judge the
Israelites (see Exodus 18:13-26), God anointed other men and women
to help Moses build the Tabernacle:

*And the Lord spake unto Moses, saying, See I have called
by name Bezaleel the son of Uri, the son of Hur, of the tribe
of Judah: And I have filled him with the spirit of God, in wisdom,
and in understanding, and in knowledge, and in all manner of
workmanship . . . And I, behold, I have given with him Aholiab,
the son of Ahisamach, of the tribe of Dan: and in the hearts
of all that are wise hearted I have put wisdom, that they may
make all that I have commanded thee . . . according to all that
I have commanded thee shall they do (Exodus 31:1-6,11).*

Not only did God anoint certain people, He also gave them some
very specific things to do. Here is what He said:

*Speak unto the children of Israel, that they bring me an
offering: of every man that giveth it willingly with his heart
ye shall take my offering. And this is the offering which ye
shall take of them; gold, and silver, and brass, And blue,
and purple, and scarlet, and fine linen, and goats' hair,
And rams' skins dyed red, and badgers' skins, and shittim
wood, Oil for the light, spices for anointing oil, and for
sweet incense, Onyx stones, and stones to be set in the
ephod, and in the breastplate (Exodus 25:2-7).*

Notice God said *every man that giveth it willingly with his heart.*
God was so meticulous in His instructions to Moses concerning the
Tabernacle that He even specified how the Israelites were supposed
to give! The people from whom Moses could accept an offering had
to have a certain heart attitude. If they didn't give willingly from the
heart, God did not want their offerings.

The concept of how serious our giving is to God is reiterated
in the New Testament: *Every man according as he purposeth in his
heart, so let him give; not grudgingly, or of necessity: for God loveth
a cheerful giver* (II Corinthians 9:7).

So the people gave willingly—all of the gold, brass, fabrics, and other things needed to build the Tabernacle. Hearts were stirred to help because they wanted the presence of God around them. They knew then, as we do today, just one touch or glimpse of God's glory would forever change them.

IN THE BEGINNING

From the beginning, God's desire was to dwell among man. Adam and Eve walked and talked with God, and dwelt with Him in the Garden of Eden, a place God had especially prepared for them to enjoy fellowship with one another.

This changed, however, when Adam and Eve sinned and partook of the tree of the knowledge of good and evil:

> *And they heard the voice of the LORD God walking in the garden in the cool of the day: and Adam and his wife hid themselves from the presence of the LORD God amongst the trees of the garden* (Genesis 3:8).

Adam and Eve didn't realize there is no place where anyone can hide from God. The psalmist wrote, *If I ascend up into heaven, thou art there: if I make my bed in hell, behold, thou art there* (Psalm 139:8). However, the consequences of Adam and Eve's behavior was their banishment from the Garden, synonymous with banishment from God's presence.

Enoch is another Old Testament believer who walked with God. God so delighted in Enoch's presence that He translated him from earth to heaven: *And Enoch walked with God: and he was not; for God took him* (Genesis 5:24).

The Greek definition of the word, *translated,* is to "transfer (i.e., life), transport, exchange, change sides," which gives us an excellent picture of what happened to Enoch. Hebrews 11:6 says faith pleases God. Because of the depth of Enoch's walk with the Father, he bypassed death and stepped into another realm of being. Enoch now enjoys an eternal presence with God that we can only look forward to and imagine:

> *By faith Enoch was translated that he should not see death; and was not found, because God had translated him: for before his translation he had this testimony, that he pleased God* (Hebrews 11:5).

God also walked and talked with Noah. At the beginning of Genesis 6, God can be found repenting for having created man, and was grieved in His heart because of the wickedness of His creation. God's presence could not dwell with man because *every imagination of the thoughts of his heart was only evil continually* (**Genesis 6:5**). But God did not turn His back on all of mankind; He chose to spare Noah and his family, because *Noah was a just man and perfect in his generations, and Noah walked with God"* (**Genesis 6:9**).

These are just a few of the Old Testament believers with whom the presence of God dwelled. There is not enough space here to write about the great men and women of old— Abraham, Isaac, and Jacob; David and Solomon; Elijah and Elisha; Esther, Ruth, and Deborah—who experienced the presence of God. One thing is certain: from Genesis to Revelation, the plan of God was to abide with His creation.

OLD TESTAMENT HABITATIONS

The Tabernacle Moses built was not the only man-made place where God chose to dwell. King David desired to build a house for God, saying, *"Lo, I dwell in an house of cedars, but the ark of the covenant of the LORD remaineth under curtains"* (**I Chronicles 17:1**).

God refused David's offer because David was a man of war, having shed blood in the sight of God. Instead, God built David a house (see I Chronicles 17:10) and promised to *raise up thy seed* [Solomon] *after thee* (**I Chronicles 17:11**).

In I Chronicles 22:6-10, David gave Solomon God's charge:

> *Then he called for Solomon his son, and charged him to build an house for the LORD God of Israel. And David said to Solomon, My son, as for me, it was in my mind to build an house unto the name of the LORD my God: But the word of the LORD came to me, saying, Thou hast shed blood abundantly, and hast made great wars: thou shalt not build an house unto my name, because thou hast shed much blood upon the earth in my sight.*
>
> *Behold, a son shall be born to thee, who shall be a man of rest; and I will give him rest from all his enemies round about: for his name shall be Solomon, and I will give peace and quietness unto Israel in his days.*

He shall build an house for my name. . .

Although God's desire is to dwell with man, He will not dwell in just any place. He demands a pure and holy vessel to inhabit. When David conceived in his heart to build the Lord a dwelling place, God gave him a "pattern" for the Temple, just like He had given the Tabernacle pattern to Moses. First Chronicles 28:12 says that David received God's pattern *by the spirit.*

Solomon was the wisest man to ever live, yet he acknowledged his human frailty when he sought God for help; and just as God had made the necessary provisions for Moses to build the Tabernacle, He did the same for Solomon:

> *But who is able to build him an house, seeing the heaven and heaven of heavens cannot contain him? Who am I then, that I should build him an house . . .? Send me now therefore a man cunning to work in gold, and in silver, and in brass, and in iron, and in purple, and crimson, and blue . . .* (II Chronicles 2:6-7).

God is no respecter of persons. At its completion, the Tabernacle was enveloped with the presence of God so powerful no one could stand. Likewise, Solomon's Temple, once completed, was met with the same overpowering presence filling its space:

> *. . . then the house was filled with a cloud, even the house of the LORD; So that the priests could not stand to minister by reason of the cloud: for the glory of the LORD had filled the house of God* (II Chronicles 5:13-14).

NEW HABITATIONS

God sent His Son to earth so man could experience His presence, not as Old Testament believers did in tents, temples, and tabernacles but through the indwelling presence of the Holy Spirit. If you are born again, the presence and power of God is in *you*! You're a walking tabernacle, and God is ever present to lead, protect, and guide you regardless of where you go or what you're doing. First Corinthians 3:16 says, *Know ye not that ye are the temple of God, and that the Spirit of God dwelleth in you?*

In John 14, Jesus told His disciples that even though He was going to return to heaven, they would not be without His presence. He would not leave them comfortless, but promised to send them the Holy Spirit Who would lead and guide them into all truth. This promise was fulfilled in Acts 2 when the disciples were baptized with the Holy Spirit and the presence of God filled them. It was at this point that God's presence began to *tabernacle* with man.

Psalm 22:3 says that God inhabits the praises of His people. Simply put, this means God inhabits everything we do to glorify Him. Adam and Eve lived in a garden, and the presence of God was there. The Israelites lived in a tent, so God said, "Put me in a tent." When His people built a temple, God said, "Put me in a temple." Finally, God said, "Put me in people so that I can be with them all of the time."

I remember years ago when my family was having a lot of problems. My father was having a nervous breakdown and there was a lot of turmoil in our home. I was engaged to my husband at that time. He brought me home one night; and when we entered my house, we felt such a presence of God. I wondered why God's presence was so strong, but then I remembered that my mother and her friends had been praying in our home. I believe God wanted us to know that in spite of everything we were going through, He was in the midst of it all and would bring us through triumphantly.

Many people can name times when they've experienced God's presence. This can happen everywhere—I've experienced the presence of God in airports and on airplanes. For some, God may have manifested His presence at church, in their cars, while they were preparing dinner, or getting ready for work. One thing is certain, God's presence can be felt.

When we look at the Tabernacle today, we're not looking at something Moses conjured up. God is the architect. When He gave Moses the blueprint, he was on Mount Sinai. In a similar way, God has a pattern for our lives, but we have to go up on the mountain where the presence of God is to find out the pattern He has for us. Then, when we come down, we have to follow that pattern to fulfill God's purpose for us. As He did with Moses, God will lead and guide us and bring the provision, people, and other things necessary to carry out His assignment.

God made every provision for Moses. The book of Exodus tells us God anointed men to do the brass work, as well as the silver and gold. God also filled women with the Spirit to embroider the linen curtains and perform the other fine work.

Moses was not alone. God gave him the pattern for the Tabernacle and then told him to go down from the mountain and carry it out. God is speaking the same to His Church today. He's saying, "You'll never stand alone in the pattern I have for your life. I will bring different people to help you do what I've called you to do."

The Body of Christ is called to work together in a pattern. Ephesians 4:16 speaks of the Body being *fitly joined together.* The Israelites pieced together a pattern. Every man, woman, boy, and girl was an important part to the building of the Tabernacle. Moses was the one to whom God gave the plan, but all of the others helped carry it out. In like manner, God has a plan for your life, one you will live out as you obey the instructions of His pattern.

Jesus told His disciples, *In my Father's house are many mansions . . .* **(John 14:2).** If you look at that passage of Scripture carefully, it is saying there are many "placements," and God has a placement for you and me. That's the place we want to find and where we want to move so we can occupy to the fullest what He has for us.

Israel took the Tabernacle with her every place she went—symbolic of the Holy Spirit in believers today. She packed it all up very carefully. God had certain people who carried the Tabernacle and its equipment. When the cloud that led them came to a halt, they didn't set up their tents first; they set up the Tabernacle—God's presence.

Revelation speaks of a time when God will once again descend from heaven and establish a resting place among men:

> *And I saw a new heaven and a new earth: for the first heaven and the first earth were passed away; and there was no more sea. And I John saw the holy city, new Jerusalem, coming down from God out of heaven, prepared as a bride adorned for her husband. And I heard a great voice out of heaven saying, Behold, the tabernacle of God is with men, and he will dwell with them, and they shall be his people, and God himself shall be with them, and be their God (Revelation 21:1-3).*

You may wonder what significance the Tabernacle plays in our society today. The answer is quite simple: God has chosen to put His presence in *you*—His tabernacle. As the Old Testament Tabernacle pointed all those who saw it to Jesus, even so should you point all those who meet you to the Lord Jesus Christ. According to 1 Corinthians 6:19, you are the temple of the Holy Spirit. You have all the power of heaven living within you. What are you doing with it?

Notes

Notes

Notes

Notes

Chapter 2

THE TABERNACLE ILLUSTRATES THREE BIBLICAL TRUTHS

In Chapter 1, we looked at the reason we should study the Tabernacle. We discovered that the Tabernacle is a *type* and *shadow* of Jesus Christ, giving a picture of Jesus in the Old Testament and a pattern for Christian life today.

The purpose of this chapter is to examine the Biblical truths the Tabernacle illustrates. By Biblical truths, I am referring to three things: 1) the Tabernacle as God's dwelling place, 2) God in Christ, reconciling man unto Himself, and 3) communion, the remembrance of Christ, all of which are revealed in the symbolism of this heavenly structure.

A RESTING PLACE

Although to some, the Tabernacle may be just another structure built by the Israelites and Moses, the Tabernacle actually illustrates heaven. It was an Old Testament picture of the New Testament indwelling of the Holy Spirit. Jesus had not yet come to earth to die for our sins, neither had He been resurrected, nor the Holy Spirit sent to abide with us. Therefore, God devised a way for His presence to dwell with man, thus giving an illustration of His Kingdom in heaven.

Hebrews 9:21-22 speaks of the Old Testament Tabernacle, in which Moses *sprinkled with blood both the tabernacle, and all the vessels of ministry. And almost all things are by the law purged with blood; and without shedding of blood is no remission.*

As I mentioned previously, the first Biblical truth has to do with a *dwelling*, or resting place for the presence of God. There's a lot of symbolism involved here. New Testament believers can stand before God today only because of the blood Jesus shed for us on Calvary. When we approach God's throne, He doesn't see our unholiness or unrighteousness. Instead, He sees our righteousness or right standing with Him through Jesus' blood.

Hebrews 10:19-20 says, *Having therefore, brethren, boldness to enter into the holiest by the blood of Jesus, By a new and living way, which he hath consecrated for us . . .* As we know from reading the Scriptures, the Israelites could not boldly approach the throne of grace. They feared God and viewed Him as a God of judgment and therefore, unapproachable. At one point, they told Moses, *Speak thou with us, and we will hear: but let not God speak with us, lest we die* (Exodus 20:19).

To get to God, the Children of Israel had to go through what some would consider an obstacle course. An example of this is the brazen altar, which I will discuss more at length in Chapter 4.

The first piece of furniture the Israelites saw when they entered the Tabernacle was the brazen altar. The altar was made of brass, which is symbolic of judgment. It was the largest and most important piece of all the Tabernacle furniture because it was where the blood sacrifice was made.

The brazen altar pointed to Jesus and foretold His Crucifixion and the shedding of His blood for the remission of our sins. The Israelites, like believers today, could not enter into God's presence or partake of His provision without coming through the blood.

Unlike Moses, the nation of Israel could never approach God directly because they were unholy and had to offer a blood sacrifice every time they wanted to atone for their sins. The priest acted as their mediator— a type of Jesus—who stood between God and the people. Only after God had accepted their sacrifice from the priest's hands, could their sins be covered, or washed, in the blood, so they could stand before the Father without fear or intimidation.

MINISTRY OF RECONCILIATION

The second Biblical truth has to do with reconciliation between God and man. The Tabernacle illustrates a type of Jesus or a heavenly place where God meets with man, reconciling him to Himself.

A definition of the word, *reconcile,* is "to reestablish friendship between." One of the reasons God wanted His presence to dwell with man is because He wanted to reestablish the relationship lost in the Garden of Eden when Adam and Eve sinned. Prior to their fall, they were "friends" with God. God owned the earth and everything in it. He chose to give Adam and Eve the title deed to the earth, transferring to them dominion over every living thing.

Adam and Eve's transgression stripped God of His right to reside on earth, giving this title deed, instead, to an illegitimate stepfather—satan! God will not violate His Word. Rather than strong-arm the devil and usurp the dominion given to him by man, God chose to manifest His presence on earth in another fashion. We see God's plan evolving in the pages of Scripture—at first His presence would temporarily come upon man, then He began to dwell in tents, tabernacles, and temples, until finally He sent the Holy Spirit to dwell within the hearts of His creation.

God gave Moses a plan mirroring the Tabernacle in heaven. Known today as the plan of salvation, God, through the Tabernacle, was reconciling man back unto Himself through the various blood sacrifices and the Aaronic priesthood. Second Corinthians 5:19 speaks of this reconciliation:

> *To wit, that God was in Christ, reconciling the world unto himself, not imputing their trespasses unto them; and hath committed unto us the word of reconciliation.*

Just as the High Priest stood before God on behalf of man, we, too, have been given the ministry of reconciliation. God's charge to the Body today is to allow His presence that is *tabernacling* in us to point all men to Jesus Christ.

WORD MADE FLESH

The Tabernacle was also a type of the "Word made flesh," as it was symbolic of Jesus' atoning work that took place when he left His home in heaven. He came to earth as a sacrificial offering to God for man, thus reconciling us back to the Father.

The book of John begins by declaring Christ as eternal:

> *In the beginning was the Word, and the Word was with God, and the Word was God. The same was in the beginning with God. . . . And the Word was made flesh, and dwelt among us . . . (John 1:1-2,14).*

From Genesis to Revelation, one of the "physical" ways God manifested His presence was in the form of a cloud and fire. In Chapter 1, we established that the presence of God led the Israelites by a pillar of cloud by day, and a pillar of fire by night. Exodus 24:17-18 speaks of the fire and the cloud that appeared as God spoke to Moses:

And the sight of the glory of the LORD was like
devouring fire on the top of the mount . . .
And Moses went into the midst of the cloud . . .

Jesus, as the "Word made flesh," could be seen each time God's presence appeared over the Tabernacle. The cloud and the fire were physical—or fleshly—manifestations God used to point man back to Himself.

COMMUNION

The third Biblical truth has to do with communion. The Tabernacle illustrated a type of communion with God. By communion, I am not referring to just fellowshipping or communing with the Father. No, the Tabernacle illustrated something that went much deeper than a superficial relationship. It spoke of consecrating oneself for God's service, and becoming one with Him.

To *consecrate* means "to set apart." The Tabernacle illustrated to the Israelites, as well as New Testament believers, the importance of separating oneself from idols, the unsaved, and the unclean. Paul admonished the Corinthian believers not to be unequally yoked, but to separate themselves from everything that was not of God:

Be ye not unequally yoked together with unbelievers:
for what fellowship hath righteousness with unrighteous-
ness? and what communion hath light with darkness? And
what concord hath Christ with Belial? or what part hath he
that believeth with an infidel? And what agreement hath
the temple of God with idols? for ye are the temple of the
living God; as God hath said, I will dwell in them, and walk
in them; and I will be their God, and they shall be my people.
Wherefore come out from among them, and be ye separate,
saith the Lord, and touch not the unclean thing; and I will
receive you (II Corinthians 6:14-17).

Because the Israelites did not have the power of the Holy Spirit at work within them to help them overcome, they would give animal sacrifices as offerings to atone for their sins. Consecrating themselves to God was a continual process, much like it is for believers today. There were five different offerings the Tabernacle priests made for the Israelites, all of which illustrated a type of consecration or communion with God (see Leviticus 1-9).

BURNT OFFERING

The five offerings offered in the Tabernacle were important because they symbolized the provisions Jesus made for us when He offered His body as a sacrifice on the Cross.

The first offering the Israelites made was the burnt offering. It has always been strange to me how the burnt offering would come first. I would have made the sin or trespass offering first. However, the burnt offering was a consecration offering. When the children of Israel entered the outer court with their burnt offering, they were saying to God, "I am consecrating myself and my substance to You."

In offering Himself on the Cross, Jesus consecrated Himself to God to do His will, and to us to become the sacrifice for our sins. He didn't have to sacrifice Himself, but He did, saying, *O my Father, if it be possible, let this cup pass from me: nevertheless not as I will, but as thou wilt* (Matthew 26:39). When Peter told Jesus, "This will never happen to you!" Jesus' response to him was, *Get thee behind me, Satan* (Matthew 16:22-23). Jesus understood why He had come to the earth, and He willingly became a burnt, or consecrated, offering for us, once and for all.

PEACE OFFERING

The peace offering was a form of celebration for the Israelites and included the entire family and their friends. They would bring an animal for sacrifice and place it on top of the brazen altar and roast it. The priest would receive his portion of the sacrifice, then the mother of the family would set a table that was soon filled with family and friends for a meal celebrating the family's peace with God. Ephesians 2:13-14 says:

> *But now in Christ Jesus ye who sometimes were far off are made nigh by the blood of Christ. For he is our peace, who hath made both one, and hath broken down the middle wall of partition between us . . .*

The Israelites did not bring the offering to *get* peace. No, they brought it to *celebrate* the peace they already had with the Father. They would say, "I've had a wonderful answer to prayer," or, "God's done something very supernatural, and I want to express how happy I am. I want to celebrate His peace, but I don't want to do it by myself."

Jesus was our peace offering. There is not peace outside of Him. The night He was born, the angels sang, *Glory to God in the highest, and on earth peace, good will toward men* (Luke 2:14). In Isaiah 9:6 He is referred to as "*The Prince of Peace*," and in John 14:27, Jesus decreed peace upon His disciples: *Peace I leave with you, my peace I give unto you . . .*

MEAL OFFERING

The meal offering had to do with the Israelites giving of their substance and God prospering them. The Apostle Paul wrote, *For ye know the grace of our Lord Jesus Christ, that, though he was rich, yet for your sakes he became poor, that ye through his poverty might be rich* (II Corinthians 8:9). Like the other offerings, the meal offering served as a *type* of abun-dant life that Jesus' death, burial, and resurrection made available to all born-again believers.

SIN & TRESPASS OFFERINGS

The sin and trespass offerings were two of the most important offerings because they dealt with transgressions and sin against God and others. The word *sin* means to "miss the mark." The sin offering was made when the Is-raelites had sinned against God. The blood of their animal sacrifices atoned for their sins and put them once again in right standing with God.

Tresspass, on the other hand, means to "go over the mark." The tres-pass offering was made when the Israelites had hurt someone, or trespassed against them. Again, it took the blood of their animal sacrifices to reconcile them both to the person they'd trespassed against, as well as to God.

So, there were sin offerings which covered their sin when they missed the mark, and trespass offerings when they overstepped the mark. James 4:7-8 says, *"Submit yourselves therefore to God. Resist the devil, and he will flee from you. Draw nigh to God, and he will draw night to you . . .* Sometimes we get so hung up on the devil, we either overstep or comp-letely miss our mark and ignore God's instructions for the best life we could have. When we're filled with love and hungry for God, the devil won't be a problem to us because we'll have a bigger solution—Jesus Christ.

Like the Israelites, in order to enter into God's presence, we have to be consecrated. Many times people are led by the Spirit but aren't receiv-ing revelation from the Word because they've forgotten this important step. If you look at the Cross, you'll see it points up and out. It points up so we might get right with God, and out so we might get right with mankind.

Jesus said that He would be the sacrifice and the provision. When we look at the Tabernacle, we see a picture of Who Jesus is to us and through us. The number five is the number of grace. Because of the grace of God, we—like the Israelites and their five offerings—can consecrate ourselves to God and have all of our needs met in Christ Jesus. Because of God's grace, we can experience His peace and be forgiven our trespasses and sins. The Tabernacle is a beautiful unfolding of Jesus Christ.

PERSONAL APPLICATION

I have a cousin who was the only one saved in his family. While my cousin was at a family reunion, one of his brothers was upset over his crops because it hadn't rained. It looked like he was going to lose literally thousands of dollars because of the drought. That night as they sat at the table, the host brought out the alcohol. My relative said, "I'm a Christian, and I feel like God teaches against drinking." His family was pretty turned off. However, when he was told about the danger of his brother losing his crops, he said, "Let's pray."

His relatives looked at him like he was a nut. However, they did allow him to pray. The brother who so desperately needed it to rain called his wife and asked her for the weather forecast. She said no rain was in sight for the next ten days.

At 5:30 the next morning, the brother's wife called to report that they'd had a tremendous rain the previous night. The next morning at the breakfast table, he said, "I want to tell you, it rained for 3 ½ hours!"

The relatives and the brother who needed the rain remembered my cousin had prayed. We may be different because of our consecration, but without a consecration, the world won't see a difference.

You may pray and read your Bible, but if you're not set apart and sanctified, you're not any different from those who don't have a relationship with Christ. If you're not consecrated and behave the same way they do by losing your temper and having pity parties, they won't see anything that can change or transform their lives. The burnt offering was the offering of consecration. Before we can enter into the presence of God's Tabernacle, we need to let the "Holy of Holies" get inside us and transform us from the inside out!

The Tabernacle Syllabus
Section 1

Notes

Notes

Notes

Notes

Chapter 3

THE CROSS: THE LAYOUT OF THE TABERNACLE

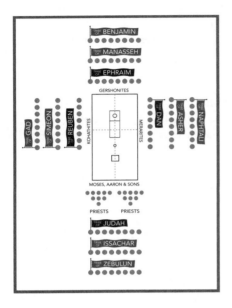

We know from studying the two previous chapters that the Tabernacle was not just another gathering place or place of trade and business. The Tabernacle was built for a specific purpose—for God's presence to inhabit, thus allowing Him to dwell among His people.

The Tabernacle was a *type* and *shadow* of Jesus Christ. One of the most striking and unique things about it was that it was shaped like a cross. The shape and arrangement of the furniture as well as the placement of the twelve tribes of Israel encamped around it, formed a cross, which foretold Christ's crucifixion, the blood He would shed on Calvary, and that God was, in the Tabernacle, a type of Christ reconciling man unto Himself.

The Tabernacle was the center of Israel's life in the wilderness, just as Christ should be the center of believers' lives today. From sun up to sun down, everything revolved around the Tabernacle. The Israelites were trained to keep their eyes on the pillars of cloud and fire, which hovered over the Tabernacle day and night. In today's terminology, we'd say the Israelites were taught to be led by the Spirit.

The pillar of cloud was a type of Holy Spirit to Old Testament believers. Just as the Holy Spirit leads us today (through an inner witness, prompting, or still small voice), in the Old Testament, the cloud was the manifested presence of God. Whenever the cloud lifted from its resting place over the Tabernacle and led Israel to yet another location in the wilderness, the Israelites would unpack and set up the Tabernacle first, even before they would set up their own tents:

> And when the cloud was taken up from the tabernacle,
> then after that the children of Israel journeyed: and in the
> place where the cloud abode, there the children of Israel
> pitched their tents. At the commandment of the LORD
> the children of Israel journeyed, and at the command-
> ment of the LORD they pitched: as long as the cloud
> abode upon the tabernacle they rested in their tents
> (Numbers 9:17-18).

The reason Israel unpacked the Tabernacle first was a strategic one—its position determined the location for each tribe. They each had a designated place around the Tabernacle, similar to the Body of Christ today. In his keen understanding of the Body of Christ and the Word of God, the Apostle Paul wrote in Ephesians 4:16, *From whom the whole body fitly joined together and compacted by that which every joint supplieth, according to the effectual working in the measure of every part . . .* and in I Corinthians 12:14,18, *"For the body is not one member, but many. . . . But now hath God set the members every one of them in the body, as it hath pleased him."*

There were three tribes to the east of the Tabernacle, three to the west, three to the north, and three to the south. God instructed Moses on the precise placement of each tribe's camp around the Tabernacle:

> And the LORD spoke unto Moses and unto Aaron,
> saying, Every man of the children of Israel shall pitch
> by his own standard, with the ensign of their father's
> house: far off about the tabernacle of the congrega-
> tion shall they pitch (Numbers 2:1-2).

It's beautiful to see the prototype God established through the pattern of the Tabernacle. First Corinthians 14:40 says, *Let all things be done decently and in order.* When Jesus fed the 5,000 in John 6, He had everyone sit down. Once he had established order, He then instructed the disciples to distribute food to the multitude. Likewise, there was a divine order in Israel's encampment around the Tabernacle:

And on the east side toward the rising of the sun
shall they of the standard of the camp of Judah pitch
throughout their armies . . . And those that do pitch
next unto him shall be the tribe of Issachar . . . Then
the tribe of Zebulun . . . On the south side shall be
the standard of the camp of Reuben . . . And those
which pitch by him shall be the tribe of Simeon . . .
Then the tribe of Gad . . . On the west side shall be
the standard of the Camp of Ephraim . . . And by him
shall be the tribe of Manasseh . . . Then the tribe of
Benjamin . . . The standard of the camp of Dan shall
be on the north side . . . And those that encamp by
him shall be the tribe of Asher . . . Then the tribe of
Naphtali . . . (Numbers 2:3, 5, 7, 10, 12, 14, 18, 20,
22, 25, 27, 29).

What would have happened if Israel had disobeyed God's order? I believe God's presence would not have dwelled among them. The "cloud" probably would have been nonexistent, faint, or sporadic in its manifestation. Many Christians experience this today. Because they ignore God's instructions, they hinder or completely stop the leading and presence of the Holy Spirit.

One time, we started a street chapel in a certain area in Denver before Teen Challenge was established there. (Teen Challenge is an organization that works with young drug addicts.) We had a real burden to minister to this segment of the population in Denver.

We went out night after night. We'd go into the streets and witness to the young people, bring them back to the chapel, and give them coffee or punch. We had an area in the back of the chapel where we'd pray for them if they wanted prayer, or they could sit at a table and talk with a Christian counselor.

We didn't know it, but we were right in the middle of an area where a large concentration of homosexuals lived. We kept wondering what was going on. Our Church began to experience difficulty, and people started coming to church with sexual problems.

My husband Wally and I became weary of the whole thing because it seemed like every time we turned around, another problem that seemed worse than the previous one was staring us in the face. One day while praying, I said, "Lord, I don't know how to handle this." The Lord spoke to me and said, "Marilyn, you'd better depend on Me to handle this one. Some of these young people really need help in this area."

We obeyed God and began to rely on Him. We were able to help many as we ministered, and God delivered some of the young people during that time. In fact, one of them attends our church today. A Teen Challenge center was opened as a result of our work. I praise God that we were obedient.

TRIBES AND BANNERS

> *And on the east side toward the rising of the sun shall*
> *they of the standard of the camp of Judah pitch throughout*
> *their armies . . . And those that do pitch next to him shall*
> *be the tribe of Issachar . . . Then the tribe of Zebulun . . .*
> *These shall first set forth* (Numbers 2:3, 5, 7, 9).

Judah, Issachar, and Zebulun camped on the east side of the Tabernacle. Judah was the "lead" tribe, in that he was located closest to the Tabernacle. With each set of tribes, a banner or ensign was erected, which acted as a guide for people. All they had to do was locate their flag, and they'd know to which side of the Tabernacle they belonged.

The three tribes on the eastern side erected a banner with the sign of a lion on it, which was the insignia for the tribe of Judah. This is significant in that the lion symbolized Jesus, Who is known as the Lion of the tribe of Judah. In the book of Matthew, Jesus is revealed as a lion, and we see the lion nature of Christ—the One triumphant King who has overcome.

There was only *one* door into the Tabernacle, and that was accessed only through the tribe of Judah. *Judah* means "praise," so what the Holy Spirit was signifying was that the Israelites must *Enter into his gates* [the Tabernacle—God's presence] *with thanksgiving, and into his courts with praise . . .* (Psalms 100:4).

Just as there is only one way to approach God today, so it was also during the Old Testament. Jesus said in John 10:9, *I am the door . . .* and in John 14:6, *I am the way . . . no man cometh unto the Father, but by me.* If New Testament believers are going to approach God, we must come through Jesus because He is the only Way.

SON OF MAN

> *On the south side shall be the standard of the camp of*
> *Reuben . . . And those which pitch by him shall be the*

> *tribe of Simeon . . . Then the tribe of Gad . . . And they*
> *shall set forth in the second rank* (Numbers 2:10,12,14,16).

The tribes to the south of the Tabernacle were Reuben, Simeon, and Gad. Their symbol was the sign of man. The gospel writers, Luke and John, reveal a dual nature of Christ. In Luke, He is revealed as the Son of Man, and His humanity can be seen throughout Luke's writings. This is why Hebrews 4:15 says Jesus can be *touched with the feeling of our infirmities* because He came to earth in the physical form of a man and was tempted in all things the same way we are, but He stayed without sin.

THE OX

> *On the west side shall be the standard of the camp of*
> *Ephraim . . . and by him shall be the tribe of Manasseh*
> *. . . Then the tribe of Benjamin . . . And they shall go forward*
> *in the third rank* (Numbers 2:18, 20, 22, 24).

To the west of the Tabernacle dwelt Ephraim, Manasseh, and Benjamin. The symbol was the ox. When I think of an ox, I envision a laboring animal that is used to tread corn. We know that Jesus was a servant to man. He said He did not come to be waited upon, but to serve all humanity. Throughout the book of Mark, Jesus is seen serving, which was a part of His earthly ministry.

THE EAGLE

> *The standard of the camp of Dan shall be on the north side*
> *. . . And those that encamp by him shall be the tribe of Asher . . .*
> *Then the tribe of Naphtali . . . They shall go hindmost with their*
> *standards* (Numbers 2:25, 27, 29, 31).

Dan, Asher, and Naphtali were located on the north side of the Tabernacle. Their symbol was the sign of an eagle. The book of John portrays Jesus as an eagle—divine, as the Son of God over all things.

THE GOSPELS

You might say, "Marilyn, why are you making such a big deal about the location and banners of the twelve tribes?" The answer is quite simple. The banners were symbolic of the four gospels—Matthew, Mark, Luke, John—revealing the fourfold ministry of Jesus Christ. Even during the prophet Ezekiel's day, the fourfold ministry of Christ can be seen, as we see in Ezekiel 1:4-5,10:

> *And I looked, and, behold, a whirlwind came out of the
> north, a great cloud, and a fire infolding itself . . . out of
> the midst thereof came the likeness of four living creatures.
> . . . As for the likeness of their faces, they four had the face
> of a man, and the face of a lion, on the right side: and they
> four had the face of an ox on the left side; they four also
> had the face of an eagle.*

And in Revelation, we read John's vision of God's throne and the
four beasts encamped around it:

> *And before the throne there was a sea of glass like unto
> crystal: and in the midst of the throne, and round about
> the throne, were four beasts . . . And the first beast was
> like a lion, and the second beast like a calf [ox], and the
> third beast had a face as a man, and the fourth beast
> was like a flying eagle* (Revelation 4:6-7).

As I've said before, no matter how you look at the Tabernacle, it points
all who see it to Jesus. This is important because it is through Christ and His
redemptive work on the Cross that we can enter into God's presence and
experience His glory. We can't be reconciled unto the Father without the
Cross of Jesus Christ: *And that he might reconcile both unto God in one
body by the cross, having slain the enmity thereby . . .* (Ephesians 2:16).

THE DOCTRINE OF BALAAM

The fact that the encampment of the Israelites was in the shape of a
cross was probably insignificant to them because they had no concept of
the Cross or Calvary at that time, which is like many of us today—sometimes
unable to see the Cross or Christ in the Old Testament or the Tabernacle
until we begin to study the Word and allow the Holy Spirit to reveal it
to us.

Balaam was an Old Testament prophet who knew God. Israel's enemies
knew about the Israelites wandering through the wilderness and that they
had great power with God. Every place they went, God wrought miracles
and caused their enemies to fall before them.

In Numbers 22:1-3, we are told about a king, named Balak, who'd also
heard about Israel and their God and feared them:

*And the children of Israel set forward, and pitched in
the plains of Moab on this side Jordan by Jericho. And
Balak the son of Zippor saw all that Israel had done to
the Amorites. And Moab was sore afraid of the people,
because they were many: and Moab was distressed
because of the children of Israel.*

Balak knew the story of how God had parted the Red Sea and
drowned Pharaoh and the Egyptians, thus delivering them into Israel's
hands. He decided the only way to defeat Israel was through a spiritual
means. Turning to the occult, to his heathen gods, he called upon the
prophet Balaam to curse Israel:

*Come now therefore, I pray thee, curse me this people;
for they are too mighty for me: peradventure I shall prevail,
that we may smite them, and that I may drive them out of
the land: for I wot that he whom thou blessest is blessed,
and he whom thou cursest is cursed* (Numbers 22:6).

He sent messengers and gifts to Balaam, who initially refused his offers.
God told Balaam in Numbers 22:12 that he could not curse the Israelites
because God had blessed them. Eventually, the king persuaded Balaam to
come, but after many efforts to curse Israel, Balaam only blessed them. On
his final attempt, Balaam looked up and, behold, he saw Christ in the form
of the cross—the Tabernacle:

*And when Balaam saw that it pleased the LORD to bless
Israel, he went not, as at other times, to seek for enchant-
ments, but he set his face toward the wilderness.*

*And Balaam lifted up his eyes, and he saw Israel abiding in
his tents according to their tribes; and the spirit of God came
upon him. And he took up his parable, and said, Balaam the
son of Beor hath said, and the man whose eyes are open hath
said . . . How goodly are thy tents, O Jacob, and thy tabernacles,
O Israel! . . . He couched, he lay down as a lion, and as a great
lion: who shall stir him up? Blessed is he that blesseth thee,
and cursed is he that curseth thee* (Numbers 24:1-3, 5, 9).

No matter which direction Balaam looked at Israel's encampment, he
saw the cross and could only bless—not curse—them. As New Testament
believers, we have inherited the blessings of Israel. Because we've chosen

to enter into the Tabernacle of God's presence through the blood of Jesus, we, too, are heirs of His promise. When unbelievers encounter a member of the Body of Christ, like Balaam, they should see the pattern of the Cross of Calvary pointing them to Jesus Christ.

Notes

Notes

The Tabernacle Syllabus
Section 1

Notes

Notes

Chapter 4

THE CONSTRUCTION OF THE TABERNACLE

In previous chapters, we examined the symbolism of the Tabernacle and the placement of the twelve tribes encamped around it. We discovered that everything about the Tabernacle, including the tribal placement, pointed those who saw it to the Lord Jesus Christ. We will continue that thread in this chapter as we focus our attention, for the first time, to the *inside* of the Tabernacle where the seven pieces of Tabernacle furniture were located.

Just as the placement of the twelve tribes of Israel around the Tabernacle were in the shape of a cross, so, too, was the arrangement of the furniture inside the Tabernacle. Although we will discuss these pieces of furniture in detail in Section II, the purpose of this chapter is to give you a general overview. The pieces of furniture inside the Tabernacle included the Brazen Altar, the Laver, the Table of Shewbread, the Golden Candlestick, the Altar of Incense, the Mercy Seat, and the Ark of the Covenant, all of which symbolized Christ and His provision for mankind.

TYPES OF ALTARS

There are many altars in Scripture. The first altar was probably built by God (see Genesis 3:21). After Adam and Eve sinned, they realized for the first time that they were naked, and God covered their nakedness with an animal's skin. Prior to their fall, God's glory had been their covering, but once they disobeyed God, a mere animal skin had to suffice. Some believe the animal from which the skin was taken was sacrificed by God upon an altar to atone for Adam and Eve's transgression.

The book of Genesis is filled with people who built altars to God. Abel built an altar in Genesis 4:4 when he offered *the firstlings of his flock and of the fat thereof.* Noah, after he and his family had escaped the flood, built an altar and offered a sacrifice of thanksgiving to God (see Genesis 8:20). Abraham, the father of faith, built many altars, one of which was erected in Genesis 15 when he and God cut the Abrahamic covenant.

The brazen altar was quite unique in the way it was made. Although the first altars were made out of the earth and unhewn rocks, the brazen altar was made out of shittim wood and covered with brass. Everything in the outer court where the brazen altar was located was made of brass. Because brass has to do with judgment, it was appropriate the first piece of furniture the Israelites saw, the piece of furniture on which the sacrifice was offered, was made of brass. Their sins had to be judged before they could experience God's presence.

THE BRAZEN ALTAR

The brazen altar was the first piece of furniture the Israelites saw when they entered the Outer court. The brazen altar was also the largest piece of furniture—every other piece of furniture inside the Tabernacle could practically fit inside of it. The altar became the most important piece of furniture because sacrifices were made on it. Everything in the Tabernacle was somehow connected to the brazen altar. The blood from the altar was sprinkled upon the mercy seat, and the fire from the altar was used to light the golden candlestick. Even the fire for the altar of incense and the meal for the loaves of shewbread had some part in the brazen altar. Moses gives a description of the altar in Exodus:

> And thou shalt make an altar of shittim wood, five cubits long, and five cubits broad; the altar shall be foursquare: and the height thereof shall be three cubits. And thou shalt make the horns of it upon the four corners thereof: his horns shall be of the same: and thou shalt overlay it with brass . . . all the vessels thereof thou shalt make of brass. And thou shalt make for it a grate of network of brass; and upon the net shalt thou make four brasen rings in the four corners thereof. . . . And thou shalt make staves for the altar, staves of shittim wood, and overlay them with brass. And the staves shall be put into the rings, and the staves shall be upon the two sides of the altar, to bear it. Hollow with boards shalt thou make it: as it was shewed thee in the mount, so shall they make it (Exodus 27:1-8).

HIGH AND LIFTED UP

According to historians, the brazen altar was placed upon a hill or mound because the Israelites had to go "up" to approach it, just as Jesus said he would be lifted up in John 3. The Israelites couldn't use a man-made object, such as a ladder, to climb up to the altar and place their sacrifice on it. We know from reading about the Tower of Babel in Genesis 11, that man cannot elevate himself to the same level as (or above) God.

Instead, God must come down to man, which is what God did in the Old Testament Tabernacle.

The word, *logos*, is said to mean, "the Word," or "a ladder let down to man." The Greeks are said to have had an interesting concept about God. They said, "Someday we're going to build a ladder and climb up to the heavens and be with God." However, they finally realized they could never get a ladder that long or that strong, so they changed their concept and said, "Someday God will come down to us." This concept was called *logos*, and Jesus became that logos when He became flesh and dwelled among us.

THE LAVER

The laver was the second piece of furniture the Israelites saw when they entered the Outer court. Like the brazen altar, the laver was also made of brass:

> *And the LORD spake unto Moses, saying, Thou shalt also make a laver of brass, and his foot also of brass, to wash withal . . . and thou shalt put water therein. For Aaron and his sons shall wash their hands and their feet thereat: When they go into the tabernacle of the congregation, they shall wash with water, that they die not; or when they come near to the altar to minister, to burn offering made by fire unto the Lord* (Exodus 30:17-20).

We do not know if the laver was made according to the specifications God gave Moses for the Tabernacle furniture. Moses did not record the dimensions for the laver. As a matter of fact, the laver has less descriptive information written about it than any other piece of Tabernacle furniture. What we do know, however, is that the laver contained water and was uncovered as the Israelites carried it through the wilderness. We can only assume how the Israelites carried the laver, perhaps in a wagon, because it did not have rings or poles like the brazen altar did for them to carry it.

The laver was used for cleansing. As the priest sacrificed animals on the brazen altar, his bare feet would become dirty and his hands bloody from the animals he was handling. Therefore, the laver was used to cleanse his feet and hands *before* he could enter the Holy Place to stand before God on behalf of the people. The priest would have died had he entered God's presence without ceremonially cleansing the animal's blood splattered on his body. Likewise, we must be cleansed by washing away the filth of the world with the water of the Word .

Jesus took the judgment for our sins, but because we are imperfect, we need continual cleansing as we live this Christian life. We judge ourselves with the Word—our scale, our measuring stick. Before we can enter God's presence and experience His glory, we must be cleansed from any defilement we may have picked up along the way. As the priest washed his feet and hands in preparation for entering into God's holy presence, we must prepare our hearts to enter God's presence.

THE TABLE OF SHEWBREAD

> *And thou shalt take fine flour, and bake twelve cakes thereof: two tenth deals shall be in one cake. And thou shalt set them in two rows, six on a row, upon the pure table before the LORD. And thou shalt put pure frankincense upon each row, that it may be on the bread for a memorial, even an offering made by fire unto the LORD. Every sabbath he shall set it in order before the LORD continually, being taken from the children of Israel by an everlasting covenant. And it shall be Aaron's and his sons'; and they shall eat it in the holy place: for it is most holy unto him of the offerings of the LORD made by fire by a perpetual statute (Leviticus 24:5-9).*

The shewbread was left out on the table for seven days. The priests sprinkled incense on the loaves; and after seven days, the priests and their families would eat the bread. *Shewbread* means "bread of faces." When the twelve loaves were placed in rows on the table of shewbread, they represented the twelve tribes of Israel, so each time the priests ate them, they were identifying with the needs of the people.

The table of shewbread was made according to the specifications given Moses in Exodus 25. Each loaf of bread weighed the same, made with exactly the same amount of flour. When the pillar of cloud began to lift from over the Holy of Holies, the priests were assigned to carry certain furniture. The priests who were assigned to the table of shewbread covered it with three coverings and carried it to their next destination.

THE GOLDEN CANDLESTICK

*And thou shalt make a candlestick of pure gold:
of beaten work shall the candlestick be made: his
shaft, and his branches, his bowls, his knops, and
his flowers, shall be of the same. And six branches
shall come out of the sides of it; three branches
of the candlestick out of the one side, and three
branches of the candlestick out of the other side:
Three bowls made like unto almonds, with a knop
and a flower in one branch; and three bowls made
like almonds in the other branch, with a knop and a
flower: so in the six branches that come out of the
candlestick. And in the candlesticks shall be four
bowls made like unto almonds, with their knops
and their flowers. And there shall be a knop under
two branches of the same, and a knop under two
branches of the same, and a knop under two branches of the same, according to the six branches that
proceed out of the candlestick. Their knops and
their branches shall be of the same: all it shall be
one beaten work of pure gold. And thou shalt make
the seven lamps thereof: and they shall light the lamps
thereof, that they may give light over against it. And
the tongs thereof, and the snuffdishes thereof, shall
be of pure gold. Of a talent of pure gold shall he
make it, with all these vessels (Exodus 25:31-39).*

The golden candlestick didn't hold a wax candle as our candlesticks do today; it was more of a lamp stand. Located on the south side of the Tabernacle, the candlestick had one central branch from which many branches extended. The priests were responsible for keeping continual light emitting from the candle stick, so they kept the central branch filled with oil, which would flow into the branches. Then the priests would light the branches.

One of the main functions of the golden candlestick was to provide light in the Holy of Holies. The sun gave natural light in the outer court where the brazen altar and laver were located, and when they entered the Holy of Holies where the mercy seat and the Ark of the Covenant were located, the glory of God was their light.

The candlestick was made of pure gold. You might ask, "Where on earth did the Israelites get this wealth?" The answer is quite simple— from Egypt. As the Israelites left Egypt, God gave them favor with the Egyptians who poured out their wealth upon them, so much so the Bible says Israel "spoiled" the Egyptians:

> And the children of Israel did according to the word of Moses; and they borrowed of the Egyptians jewels of silver, and jewels of gold, and raiment: And the LORD gave the people favour in the sight of the Egyptians, so that they lent unto them such things as they required. And they spoiled the Egyptians (Exodus 12:35-36).

When it came to building the Tabernacle, God stirred the Israelites' hearts to give of their best:

> Speak unto the children of Israel, that they bring me an offering: of every man that giveth it willingly with his heart ye shall take my offering. And this is the offering which ye shall take of them; gold, and silver, and brass, And blue, and purple, and scarlet, and fine linen, and goats' hair, And rams' skins dyed red, and badgers' skins, and shittim wood, Oil for the light, spices for anointing oil, and for sweet incense, Onyx stones, and stones to be set in the ephod, and in the breastplate (Exodus 25:2-7).

In fact, they gave willingly, and with such fervor, that Moses had to restrain them from giving:

> And they spake unto Moses, saying, The people bring much more than enough for the service of the work, which the LORD commanded to make. And Moses gave command-ment, and they caused it to be proclaimed throughout the camp, saying, Let neither man nor woman make any more work for the offering of the sanctuary. So the people were restrained from bringing (Exodus 36:5-6).

THE ALTAR OF INCENSE

> *And thou shalt make an altar to burn incense upon: of shittim wood shalt thou make it. A cubit shall be the length thereof, and a cubit the breadth thereof; foursquare shall it be: and two cubits shall be the height thereof: the horns thereof shall be of the same. And thou shalt overlay it with pure gold, the top thereof, and the sides thereof round about, and the horns thereof; and thou shalt make unto it a crown of gold round about. And two golden rings shalt thou make to it under the crown of it, by the two corners thereof, upon the two sides of it shalt thou make it; and they shall be for places for the staves to bear it withal. And thou shalt make the staves of shittim wood, and overlay them with gold. And thou shalt put it before the vail that is by the ark of the testimony, before the mercy seat that is over the testimony, where I will meet with thee. And Aaron shall burn thereon sweet incense every morning: when he dresseth the lamps, he shall burn incense upon it. And when Aaron lighteth the lamps at even, he shall burn incense upon it, a per-petual incense before the LORD throughout your generations (Exodus 30:1-8).*

The altar of incense was the final piece of furniture in the Holy Place. It was made of shittim wood, which was a very durable wood, and covered with gold. There was a place on the altar of incense that Aaron would light, then offer up prayers for the children of Israel.

There were two altars in the Tabernacle—the brazen altar in the Outer Court where the animals were sacrificed, and the altar of incense in the Holy Place where a different kind of sacrifice was made: prayer. Both altars had four horns, the significance of which will be discussed in a later chapter.

Fire from the brazen altar was used to burn the incense. The priest would take coals of fire from the brazen altar and put them in a cup where they would burn incense on the altar of incense. They could not bring just any coals either; doing so could cost them their lives. Aaron's two sons were examples of this. One day they decided to offer up "strange fire" unto God, and the fire of the Lord consumed them:

> *And Nadab and Abihu, the sons of Aaron, took either*
> *of them his censer, and put fire therein, and put incense*
> *thereon, and offered strange fire before the LORD, which*
> *he commanded them not. And there went out fire from*
> *the LORD, and devoured them, and they died before*
> *the LORD* (Leviticus 10:1-2).

Although the consequences of Nadab and Abihu's sin may seem harsh, God made very clear the gravity of following the pattern for the Tabernacle He had established.

THE ARK OF THE COVENANT

> *And they shall make an ark of shittim wood: two cubits*
> *and a half shall be the length thereof, and a cubit and a*
> *half the breadth thereof, and a cubit and a half the height*
> *thereof. And thou shalt overlay it with pure gold, within*
> *and without shalt thou overlay it, and shalt make upon it*
> *a crown of gold round about. And thou shalt cast four rings*
> *of gold for it, and put them in the four corners thereof; and*
> *two rings shall be in the one side of it, and two rings in the*
> *other side of it. And thou shalt make staves of shittim wood,*
> *and overlay them with gold. And thou shalt put the staves*
> *into the rings by the sides of the ark, that the ark may be*
> *borne with them. The staves shall be in the rings of the ark:*
> *they shall not be taken from it. And thou shalt put into the*
> *ark the testimony which I shall give thee* (Exodus 25:10-16).

The Ark of the Covenant was located in the Holy of Holies. It was made of wood and covered with gold. Unlike the other articles of furniture in the Tabernacle, the Ark of the Covenant contained the golden pot of manna, Aaron's rod, and the Ten Commandments. It was always covered with a veil and carried ahead of the people. When it was resting in the Holy of Holies, the priests could enter, but even then, only with an offering of blood.

The Ark of the Covenant is a beautiful reminder that the presence of God came down over the mercy seat. The Ark led and protected the Israelites, helped them win over their enemies, and gave them rest. When it was time for the Israelites to enter into the Promised Land, they took the Ark to the Jordan River, which was overflowing. When the priests stepped into the water with the Ark, the waters rolled back and stood up:

*And it came to pass, when the people removed from
their tents, to pass over Jordan, and the priests bearing
the ark of the covenant before the people; And as they
that bare the ark were come unto Jordan, and the feet
of the priests that bare the ark were dipped in the brim
of the water, (for Jordan overfloweth all his banks all the
time of harvest,) That the waters which came down from
above stood and rose up upon an heap very far from the
city Adam, that is beside Zaretan: and those that came
down toward the sea of the plain, even the salt sea, failed,
and were cut off: and the people passed over right against
Jericho. And the priests that bare the ark of the covenant
of the LORD stood firm on dry ground in the midst of
Jordan, and all the Israelites passed over on dry ground,
until all the people were passed clean over Jordan*
(Joshua 3:14-17).

The Ark did not have a permanent resting place. Instead, it resided
in a tent. It was the only piece of furniture Moses himself built. Just as the
Tabernacle was the center of Israel's life, the entire Tabernacle was built
around the Ark.

THE MERCY SEAT

*And thou shalt make a mercy seat of pure gold . . . And
thou shalt make two cherubims of gold, of beaten work
shalt thou make them, in the two ends of the mercy seat.
And make one cherub on the one end, and the other cherub
on the other end: even of the mercy seat shall ye make the
cherubims on the two ends thereof. And the cherubims shall
stretch forth their wings on high, covering the mercy seat with
their wings, and their faces shall look one to another; toward
the mercy seat shall the faces of the cherubims be. And thou
shalt put the mercy seat above upon the ark; and in the ark
thou shalt put the testimony that I shall give thee. And there
I will meet with thee, and I will commune with thee from above
the mercy seat, from between the two cherubims . . .* (Exodus
25:17-22).

The mercy seat was made of pure gold and fashioned with two
cherubims guarding the throne. The presence of God hovered over the

mercy seat between the two cherubim in the form of a pillar of cloud by day and a pillar of fire by night.

The high priest sprinkled blood on the mercy seat for the remission of sin. On the day of atonement, he would enter into the Holy of Holies and sprinkle blood seven times before the mercy seat (see Leviticus 16). It was at the mercy seat in the Holy of Holies, where God would meet with his priests and speak to them.

Notes

Notes

Notes

Notes

Chapter 5

THE PRIESTHOOD AND THE OLD TESTAMENT TABERNACLE

No place of God—church, religious organization, or otherwise—is complete without those who minister in God's stead. The Old Testament Tabernacle was no exception. Just as we've seen how everything about the Tabernacle—from the arrangement of the furniture to the placement of the twelve tribes—points to Jesus Christ, so, too, do the priests who were ordained by God to minister in the Tabernacle for the nation of Israel.

A priest is one who stands in the gap and intercedes—pleads for mercy—for others. Moses was one of the first priests God appointed to intercede for the Israelites. His priesthood began in Exodus 3 when God spoke to Him out of the burning bush:

> And the angel of the LORD appeared unto him in a flame of fire out of the midst of a bush . . . And Moses said, I will now turn aside, and see this great sight, why the bush is not burnt. And when the LORD saw that he turned aside to see, God called unto him out of the midst of the bush, and said . . . I am the God of thy father, the God of Abraham, the God of Isaac, and the God of Jacob. . . . And the LORD said, I have surely seen the affliction of my people which are in Egypt, and have heard their cry by reason of their taskmasters; for I know their sorrows; And I am come down to deliver them out of the hand of the Egyptians, and to bring them up out of that land unto a good land and a large, unto a land flowing with milk and honey . . . Come now therefore, and I will send thee unto Pharaoh, that thou mayest bring forth my people the children of Israel out of Egypt (Exodus 3:2-4, 6-8,10).

The word "priest," according to STRONG'S EXHAUSTIVE CONCORDANCE OF THE BIBLE, means *"one officiating, to do the office of a priest, to execute, to minister in the priest's office."* As we know from studying Old Testament scriptures, Moses stood in the office of a priest on numerous occasions. As a priest, he was responsible for being a mediator between God and man. In Egypt, he stood before Pharaoh, on behalf of the Israelites according to the will and instructions of God, and in Exodus, Moses literally pleaded with God to spare the lives of the entire nation of Israel:

> And the LORD said unto Moses, I have seen this people, and, behold, it is a stiffnecked people: Now therefore let me alone, that my wrath may wax hot against them, and that I may consume them: and I will make of thee a great nation. And Moses besought the LORD his God, and said, LORD, why doth thy wrath wax hot against thy people, which thou hast brought forth out of the land of Egypt with great power, and with a mighty hand? Wherefore should the Egyptians speak, and say, For mischief did he bring them out, to slay them in the mountains, and to consume them from the face of the earth? Turn from thy fierce wrath, and repent of this evil against thy people. Remember Abraham, Isaac, and Israel, thy servants, to whom thou swarest by thine own self, and saidst unto them, I will multiply your seed as the stars of heaven, and all this land that I have spoken of will I give unto your seed, and they shall inherit it for ever. And the LORD repented of the evil which he thought to do unto his people (Exodus 32:9-14).

A NATION OF PRIESTS

Just as God gave Moses the pattern for the Tabernacle and its furniture, He also gave him instructions concerning the priests, who he'd appointed to stand before Him. When God spoke to the people at Mt. Sinai, He told them that they were to be a nation of priests:

> Ye have seen what I did unto the Egyptians, and how I bare you on eagles' wings, and brought you unto myself. Now therefore, if ye will obey my voice indeed, and keep my covenant, then ye shall be a peculiar treasure unto me above all people: for all the earth is mine: And ye shall be unto me a kingdom of priests, and an holy nation. . . . (Exodus 19:4-6).

The reason God wanted the nation of Israel to be priests is because they were to be a reflection of Him. They were going to take possession of the Promised Land. Not only did God want Israel to minister unto Him, but He also wanted them to minister to the surrounding nations. However, the Israelites panicked and rejected the call of God. They told Moses, *Speak thou with us, and we will hear: but let not God speak with us, lest we die* (Exodus 20:19).

Moses stood in the gap so God would not destroy them, and instead of Israel becoming a nation of priests as God had wanted, one family was chosen from the Israelites to minister as priests before God. However, through the sacrifice of His Son, God achieved His original desire and reestablished relationship with us—the New Testament Body of Christ—*a royal priesthood, an holy nation* (I Peter 2:9).

THE PRIESTHOOD

The purpose of the priesthood in the Old Testament Tabernacle was fourfold. The priests were to take care of the Ark of the Covenant and the Tabernacle. They were also to minister unto the Lord and to hear from Him. There are several different priesthoods recorded in the Scriptures. Melchizedek is the first person referred to as a priest in the Bible. He ministered during the days of Abraham.

As a priest, he blessed Abraham, served him communion, and received his tithes:

> *And Melchizedek king of Salem brought forth bread and wine: and he was the priest of the most high God. And he blessed him, and said, Blessed be Abram of the most high God, possessor of heaven and earth: And blessed be the most high God, which hath delivered thine enemies into thy hand. And he gave him tithes of all* (Genesis 14:18-20).

The Aaronic priesthood is the next priesthood we read about in Scripture. Because the Israelites refused their calling as a nation of priests, God chose a family from the tribe of Levi to minister as priests before Him.

If you'll recall, when God called Moses to deliver Israel from the land of Egypt, Moses had many excuses why he was unqualified to fulfill God's call. After a lengthy discussion in Exodus 4, God told Moses that He would appoint his brother, Aaron, as a mouthpiece to intercede for Moses and the Israelites.

Once the Israelites had been delivered from Egypt and were well on their way to the Promised Land, God chose Aaron and his sons to act as priests and to minister in the Tabernacle before Him:

> *And take thou unto thee Aaron thy brother, and his sons with him, from among the children of Israel, that he may minister unto me in the priest's office, even Aaron, Nadab and Abihu, Eleazar and Ithamar, Aaron's sons* (Exodus 28:1).

As ministers of God, Aaron and his sons served as high priests before the Lord. The high priest, if you remember, was the only person allowed to enter the Holy Place and Holy of Holies in the Tabernacle without being struck dead.

Jesus is our High Priest today. Just as the Old Testament priests offered up sacrifices and prayers on behalf of the Israelites, Jesus . . . *after he had offered one sacrifice for sins forever, sat down on the right hand of God . . . [and He] . . . ever liveth to make intercession for them* (Hebrews 10:12, 7:25).

The Apostle Paul wrote about all three types of these priesthoods in the book of Hebrews. He refers to Jesus as our High Priest (see Hebrews 3:1), and, in Hebrews 7, compares and contrasts the Levitical priesthood of Melchizedek to that of Jesus.

Without a doubt, the priesthood is very important in the mind and heart of God. Although many people in the Old Testament stood as priests—Abraham, Noah, Job—God has ordained the New Testament church to act as priests before Him. Melchizedek, Aaron, and his sons were the types and shadows of the role we are to take today as high priests to our families, communities, cities, states, countries, and yes, even nations!

CONSECRATION

Aaron and his sons had to be consecrated before they could minister in the office of high priest. God told Moses regarding the purity of the priests, *I will be sanctified in them that come nigh me . . .* (Leviticus 10:3). They were in a place of judgment and had to judge themselves in order to minister to the Israelites coming for the forgiveness of their sins.

As previously stated, the priests offered five offerings in the Tabernacle to atone for the sins of the Israelites. Because they stood in the gap for others, it was imperative that the priests themselves be washed and cleansed.

The consecration of Aaron and his sons was for everyone to see. All of Israel came out to witness their public confession before they could minister in the office of high priest. Moses officiated at the ceremonial consecration. He anointed Aaron and his sons for God's calling, commission, cleansing, clothing, consecration, and compassion.

The word "consecrate" means to be "set apart" for a particular service or office. Just as He had given instructions about everything else concerning the Tabernacle, God also commanded Moses concerning the priests:

> *Take Aaron and his sons with him, and the garments, and the anointing oil, and a bullock for the sin offering, and two rams, and a basket of unleavened bread; And gather thou all the congregation together unto the door of the tabernacle of the congregation. And Moses did as the LORD commanded him . . . And Moses said unto the congregation, This is the thing which the LORD commanded to be done. And Moses brought Aaron and his sons, and washed them with water (Leviticus 8:2-6).*

According to Leviticus 8, the priests were taken out from among the people. They were set apart for God's service, just as we were sanctified and set apart by God when we became born again.

The priests were also brought to the door of the Tabernacle, where the congregation could witness their consecration. This was symbolic of Jesus' crucifixion at Golgotha where the multitudes gathered to see Him lay down His life for mankind.

The third thing that happened before the priests could minister before God was that they had to be washed with water. Water is a cleansing agent, and as always in the Bible, it is symbolic of the Word of God. Moses washed the priests in the door of the Tabernacle in front of the entire congregation. This was a public confirmation that Aaron and his sons were holy men, appointed by God to minister before Him.

AARON'S GARMENTS

> *And he put upon him the coat, and girded him with the girdle, and clothed him with the robe, and put the ephod upon him, and he girded him with the curious girdle of the ephod, and bound it unto him therewith. And he put the breastplate upon him: also he put in the breastplate the Urim and the Thummim. And he put the mitre upon his head; also upon the mitre, even upon his forefront, did*

he put the golden plate, the holy crown; as the LORD commanded Moses (Leviticus 8:7-9).

No washing is complete without the putting on of clothes, and so it was with the consecration of the Old Testament priests. After Moses had washed them with the washing of the water by the Word, he began to clothe them in their priestly garments. In like manner, we, too, are clothed in God's righteousness and have put off the garments of sin.

The priests were clothed with seven garments—seven is the number of completion—for the glory and honor of God. The first garment was the breastplate, which the Apostle Paul refers to in Ephesians 6:14 when he says to put on the breastplate of righteousness.

The breastplate had twelve stones in it, each engraved with the name of one of the twelve tribes of Israel. In addition there were two stones—one on each shoulder of the breastplate—with the names of the twelve tribes also engraved on them:

And thou shalt make the breastplate of judgment . . . And thou shalt set in it settings of stones, even four rows of stones: the first row shall be a sardius, a topaz, and a carbuncle . . . And the second row shall be an emerald, a sapphire, and a diamond. And the third row a ligure, an agate, and an amethyst. And the fourth row a beryl, and an onyx, and a jasper . . . And the stones shall be with the names of the children of Israel, twelve, according to their names, like the engravings of a signet; everyone with his name shall they be according to the twelve tribes (Exodus 28:15, 17-21).

The high priest wore the breastplate when he ministered to God for the twelve tribes. They were close to his heart both literally and figuratively.

Judah was engraved on the first stone, which was an emerald. If you recall, *Judah* means "praise." Judah always marched first, so praise led the Israelites each time they changed locations or went into battle.

The second stone, an amethyst was for Issachar. *Issachar* means "reward." His symbol was the ox, which is the symbol used to portray Jesus as a servant in the book of Mark. When we serve God, we are rewarded.

Zebulun was the third name engraved on this priest's breastplate, and the beryl was his stone. *Zebulun* means "dwelling." To *dwell* is another way of saying to *abide*. In John 15:7, Jesus says, *If ye abide in me, and my words abide in you, ye shall ask what ye will, and it shall be done unto you.*

The fourth name on the priest's breastplate was Reuben. His stone was the sardius. *Reuben* means "vision of the son." In other words, the Israelites were beholding a type and shadow of Jesus Christ.

Number five in line was none other than *Simeon,* which means "hearing." Israel was to have a hearing ear to listen to and understand what God was saying. The topaz was Simeon's stone.

In the Bible, the number six is the number of man. The tribe of Gad was the sixth name engraved in the breastplate, and its stone was the ligure. *Gad* stands for "blessing"—the blessings of God were multiplied upon the nation of Israel.

Ephraim was the seventh name—the number of completion—and the stone was a sapphire. *Ephraim* means "double portion." In II Kings 2:9, the prophet Elisha asked for a double portion of the prophet Elijah's spirit, and he got it.

Now, God divided Joseph's tribe into two, Manasseh and Ephraim, *For the children of Joseph were two tribes, Manasseh and Ephraim: therefore they gave no part unto the Levites in the land, save cities to dwell in, with their suburbs for their cattle and for their substance* (Joshua 14:4).

The eighth stone was the chalcedony, and Manasseh was the tribe. *Manasseh* means "causing to forget." As they journeyed through the wilderness, the Israelites were to forget the sins of the past, which the Apostle Paul spoke of when he said, *. . . forgetting those things which are behind, . . . I press toward the mark for the prize of the high calling of God in Christ Jesus* (Philippians 3:13-14).

The ninth tribe engraved on the breastplate was *Benjamin,* meaning, "son of my right hand," and his stone was the jasper. Jesus is seated at the right hand of the Father, making intercession for you and me. And we are Jesus' right hands, extended to the world as we fulfill His call to make disciples of all mankind.

Dan, "to judge," was the tenth name engraved, his stone, agate. The sins of the Israelites were judged at the brazen altar, and we are to judge ourselves instead of judging others.

The next to the last tribe was Asher, and sardonyx was his stone. *Asher* means "happy" or "happiness."

The final stone was the diamond, upon which Naphtali was engraved. *Naphtali* means "wrestling." Jacob wrestled with an angel all night until God changed his nature, and Paul tells us in Ephesians 6 that we wrestle not against flesh and blood.

One unique characteristic about the breastplate was that it had pockets in it which contained the Urim and Thummim. *Urim* and *Thummim* mean "lights" and "perfections." When an Israelite inquired of the priest for the will of God, the priest would seek the Lord in prayer. Then he would reach in his breast pocket, pull out the Urim and Thummim, and throw them in his lap. The way they fell, called the casting of lots, determined the will of God for the person inquiring.

> *And thou shalt put in the breastplate of judgment the Urim and the Thummim; and they shall be upon Aaron's heart, when he goeth in before the LORD . . . (Exodus 28:30).*

When the Israelites were ready to possess the Promised Land, the high priest cast lots to determine where each tribe would live. So the Urim and Thummim would reveal the perfect will of God for Israel's situation. Just as there was a perfect plan for each of the twelve tribes of Israel, Jesus has a perfect plan for each one of us.

THE EPHOD

The ephod was the second garment the priest wore as he ministered in the Tabernacle. Although each piece of the priest's garment was extremely important, it seems that the primary purpose of the ephod was to make sure the breastplate stayed stationary:

> *And thou shalt make two rings of gold, and thou shalt put them upon the two ends of the breastplate in the border thereof, which is in the side of the ephod inward. And two other rings of gold thou shalt make, and shalt put them on the two sides of the ephod underneath, toward the forepart thereof, over against the other coupling thereof, above the curious girdle of the ephod. And they shall bind the breastplate by the rings thereof unto the rings of the ephod with a lace of blue, that it*

*may be above the curious girdle of the ephod, and that
the breastplate be not loosed from the ephod*
(Exodus 28:26-28).

THE ROBE OF RIGHTEOUSNESS

The third garment the priest wore to minister in the Tabernacle was
a robe that had alternating pomegranates and bells along the hem. The
pomegranates symbolized peace, and the sound of the bells meant the
priest was interceding for the Israelites:

*And thou shalt make the robe of the ephod all of blue.
. . . And beneath upon the hem of it thou shalt make
pomegranates of blue, and of purple, and of scarlet,
round about the hem thereof; and bells of gold between
them round about; A golden bell and a pomegranate,
a golden bell and a pomegranate, upon the hem of the
robe round about* (Exodus 28:31,33-34).

The priests ministered in the power and character of the Holy Spirit.
The pomegranates and bells can be likened to the gifts of the Spirit in
I Corinthians 12, and the fruit of the Spirit in Galatians 5. The fruit of the
Spirit is symbolic of the character of God, and there is a fruit that goes
with each spiritual gift. The fruit of the Spirit can go hand-in-hand with the
gifts of the Spirit; for example, the fruit of love can be matched with the
gifts of healing. When we operate in the love of God, His compassion
comes forth and He is able to manifest Himself in the area of healing.
However, if we operate in the gifts without the fruit of the Spirit, we may
be able to benefit others, but our personal and spiritual lives will profit
us nothing (see I Corinthians 13:1-3).

*And thou shalt embroider the coat of fine linen, . . .
And for Aaron's sons thou shalt make coats, and thou
shalt make for them girdles, and bonnets shalt thou
make them, for glory and for beauty* (Exodus 28:39-40).

Over the top of the priest's robe was an embroidered coat, which
symbolized the putting on of Christ. The priest was also clad in a girdle,
which was used for service. It pulled up the priest's robe, as he marched
or ministered in the Tabernacle, and held it in place so he'd be free to
walk without tripping.

The priests were clothed from head to toe. Although there was no distinction between what Aaron and his sons wore with most of the garments, when it came to their headpieces, the Bible indicates that there was a definite difference. Aaron wore an engraved mitre made of pure gold, and his sons wore bonnets:

> And thou shalt make a plate of pure gold, and grave
> upon it, like the engravings of a signet, HOLINESS
> TO THE LORD. . . . And it shall be upon Aaron's
> forehead, that Aaron may bear the iniquity of the
> holy things, which the children of Israel shall hallow
> in all their holy gifts; and it shall be always upon his
> forehead, that they may be accepted before the
> LORD. . . . And for Aaron's sons . . . bonnets shalt
> thou make for them . . . (Exodus 28:36, 38, 40).

The bonnets that Aaron's sons wore were more like turbans than the traditional bonnets to which we are accustomed.

The final pieces of the priests' garments included the girdle and breeches. Although not much is said about the girdle, the priests' breeches were to cover their nakedness as they ministered before the Lord:

> And thou shalt make them linen breeches to cover
> their nakedness; from the loins even unto the thighs
> they shall reach: And they shall be upon Aaron, and
> upon his sons, when they come in unto the tabernacle
> of the congregation, or when they come near unto the
> altar to minister in the holy place; that they bear not
> iniquity, and die . . . (Exodus 28:42-43).

ANOINTING OIL

You can hardly talk about the consecration of the Tabernacle or priests without also discussing blood and the anointing oil. Both were used in the dedication of the Tabernacle and the Aaronic priesthood. Every piece of furniture in the Tabernacle was anointed with oil and blood. This was symbolic because the priests were not only to have the cleansing of the blood to make them pure, but they were also to have the anointing in order to pray and minister to God and for the people:

Then shalt thou kill the ram, and take of his blood, and put it upon the tip of the right ear of Aaron, and upon the tip of the right ear of his sons, and upon the thumb of their right hand, and upon the great toe of their right foot, and sprinkle the blood upon the altar round about. And thou shalt take of the blood that is upon the altar, and of the anointing oil, and sprinkle it upon Aaron, and upon his garments, and upon his sons, and upon the garments of his sons with him: and he shall be hallowed, and his garments, and his sons, and his sons' garments with him (Exodus 29:20-21).

God gave Moses specific instructions for how to sanctify Aaron and his sons for the priesthood. Moses anointed the tips of each of their right ear, their right thumb, and big toe of their right foot. Why? Their ears, because God wanted their hearing cleansed so they'd have an ear to hear what He was saying. Their thumbs, to perform the service of God, and the big toe on the right foot, so they could walk free of sin and according to the leading Spirit of God.

The anointing oil was similar to the manna God fed the Israelites in that it could not be reproduced. A special recipe of myrrh, cinnamon, calamus, and cassia oil (see Exodus 30:23-24) was only to be used to anoint the Tabernacle and the priests, or to burn in the altar of incense. Any use to the contrary was punishable by death.

The service and consecration of the priests in the Old Testament Tabernacle are not to be taken lightly. Just as with all of the other instructions God gave Moses concerning the Tabernacle, the specifications for the priesthood and the sanctification of the priests were just as important. As the encampment of the tribes and the arrangement of the furniture pointed all who saw them to the Lord Jesus Christ, so did the ministry and consecration of the priests. They were a *type* and *shadow* of how we are to stand before God today, as intercessors and priests of the most high God.

Notes

Notes

Notes

Notes

THE TABERNACLE
SYLLABUS

Section 2
YOUR ILLUSTRATED GUIDE THROUGH
THE TABERNACLE

CONTENTS

TABERNACLE OVERVIEW

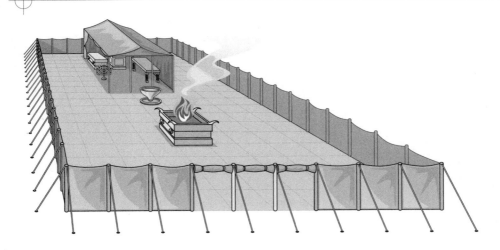

THEME VERSE: EXODUS 25:8

LOCATION: In the center of the Israelites' camp

OLD TESTAMENT SIGNIFICANCE: God wanted to Tabernacle with men.

POINTS TO JESUS: He came to earth to show us the way to the heavenly Tabernacle.

I Corinthians 3:16: *Know ye not that ye are the temple of God, and that the Spirit of God dwelleth in you?*

John 14:3: *And if I go and prepare a place for you, I will come again, and receive you unto myself; that where I am, there ye may be also.*

Outline

I. **THE CHURCH**

    A. Israel, the church in the wilderness

    B. New Testament Church in the world

II. **THE MOSAIC COVENANT**

    A. Five-fold foundation

        1. The tabernacle of Moses (Exodus 25-40)

        2. The law covenant (Exodus 20)

        3. The priesthood

            a. Aaronic

            b. Levitical (Exodus 28, 29, 30)

        4. The five offerings and sacrifices (Leviticus 1-7)

        5. The three feasts

            a. Passover

            b. Pentecost

            c. Tabernacles (Leviticus 23)

III. **THE DIVINE PURPOSE**

    A. *And let them make me a sanctuary; that I may dwell among them* (Exodus 25:8).

IV. THE SEVEN-FOLD REQUIREMENTS FOR BUILDING THE SANCTUARY

A. The dwelling place of God was to be built.

1. Freewill offerings (Exodus 25:2)

2. The "people stirred up" (Exodus 36:2)

3. Willing people (Exodus 25:1, 2)

4. Free-hearted people (Exodus 35, 36)

5. Wisdom of God (Exodus 36:1-8)

6. Spirit of God (Exodus 35:30-35)

7. Divine plan (Hebrews 8:5)

V. THE BUILDERS OF THE TABERNACLE

A. Bezaleel (Exodus 31:1-5)

B. Aholiab (Exodus 31:6)

C. The women helped.

1. Exodus 35:25: *And all the women that were wise hearted did spin with their hands, and brought that which they had spun, both of blue, and of purple, and of scarlet, and of fine linen.*

2. Exodus 35:26: *And all the women whose heart stirred them up in wisdom spun goats' hair.*

VI. THE TIME IN BUILDING

A. It was completed in nine months.

B. It was nine months of preparation for Jesus in the womb of Mary.

VII. THE TABERNACLE IN REVELATION

A. The Temple of God is heavenly (Revelation 11:1,15:5).

B. God wants to dwell with His people (Revelation 21:3).

THE OUTER COURT

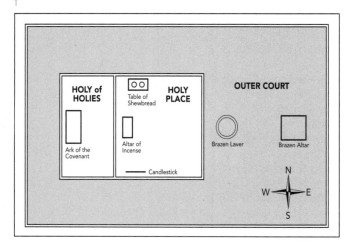

THEME VERSE: EXODUS 27:9-19

LOCATION: Oblong area surrounded by 60 pillars

OLD TESTAMENT SIGNIFICANCE: The approach to the brazen laver and the brazen altar

POINTS TO JESUS: Jesus came as Savior for all nations

Hebrews 9:28: *So Christ was once offered to bear the sins of many; and unto them that look for him shall he appear the second time without sin unto salvation.*

I. **A BARRIER THAT PRESERVED THE SANCTITY OF THE TABERNACLE**

   A. Inside was a place of righteousness.

   B. The white linen was a contrast to the black tents outside.

   C. Jesus is righteous in the midst of a perverse and crooked generation.

II. **PROTECTION FROM THE OUTSIDE THREATS**

    A.   Redemption is found within its walls.

    B.   Jesus received our judgment for us.

III. **A BARRIER BETWEEN THE WORLD AND GOD**

    A.   Man cannot approach God without a blood sacrifice.

    B.   Anyone could come into this court.

IV. **THE ONLY WAY TO APPROACH GOD**

    A.   It is a wide entrance so all can enter.

    B.   It is an attractive way and a way we cannot make for ourselves.

    C.   It is well-supported by four beautiful pillars (the four gospels).

V. **THE OUTER COURT IN REVELATION**

    A.   There is a court of the Gentiles (Revelation 11:2).

    B.   People of all nations and tongues will be before God's heavenly throne (Revelation 7:9).

THE BRAZEN ALTAR

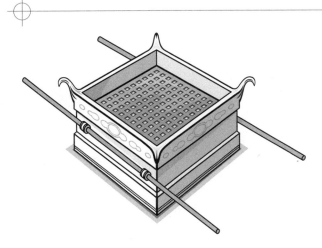

THEME VERSES: EXODUS 27:1-5

LOCATION: Outer Court

OLD TESTAMENT SIGNIFICANCE: Place of sacrifice

POINTS TO JESUS: Jesus is our Redeemer, Substitution, Reconciler.

Hebrews 7:27: *Who needeth not daily, as those high priests, to offer up sacrifice, first for his own sins, and then for the people's: for this he did once, when he offered up himself.*

(Refer to Section I, Chapter 2 in this syllabus)

I.   THE BRAZEN ALTAR IN GENERAL

    A.   Its measurements (Exodus 27:1)

    B.   Its horns (Exodus 27:2)

    C.   Made of wood and brass (Exodus 27:2)

    D.   Its vessels (Exodus 27:3)

II.   MADE BY THE SPIRIT AND WISDOM OF GOD (EXODUS 27:8)

    A.   Placed before the door of the Tabernacle (Exodus 40:6)

    B.   Its covering (Numbers 16:36-40)

    C.   Altar in transit (Numbers 3:30-31)

    D.   Divine fire (Leviticus 6:12-13)

    E.   The anointing (Exodus 30:28-29)

III. THE ASHES

    A.   Placed outside the camp in the clean place (Leviticus 6:10-11)

    B.   The unclean place was outside the camp for the plague (Leviticus 14:40)

IV. JUDGMENT ALWAYS BEGINS AT THE ALTAR (EZEKIEL 9:1-7; I PETER 4:17)

A. Altar means "to be lifted up" or "ascending"

B. The altar is the place of slaughter

V. THE HORNS OF THE ALTAR (EXODUS 27:2)

A. Horns have to do with strength.

B. The sacrifice was tied to the horns.

C. The four horns

1. Redemption

2. Ransom

3. Substitution

4. Reconciliation

VI. THE HISTORY OF OTHER ALTARS IN THE BIBLE

A. Altar of God in Eden (Genesis 3:21-24)

B. Altar of Abel at gate of Eden (Genesis 4:1-4, Hebrews 11:4)

C. Altar of Noah (Genesis 8:20)

D. Altar of Abraham (Genesis 12:7)

E. Altar of Isaac (Genesis 26:25)

F. Altar of Jacob (Genesis 35:1)

G. Moses' altar (Joshua 8:31)

H. Gideon's altar (Judges 6:24)

I. Manoah's altar (Judges 13:20)

J. Saul's first altar (I Samuel 14:35)

K. David's altar (II Samuel 24:25)

L.   Elijah repaired the altar (I Kings 18:30)

VII. THE FIVE SACRIFICES DEALT WITH CONSECRATION

A.   The burnt offering (Leviticus 1)

1.   Offered from the cattle

2.   A male without blemish killed before the door

3.   Offered voluntarily

4.   Offered on the altar as a sweet savor to the Lord

5.   Accepted by the priest as an atonement

B.   The meat/meal offering had to do with consecration of possessions (Leviticus 2).

1.   Of fine flour with oil poured on it with frankincense

2.   Made without leaven

3.   The remnant to be for Aaron and his sons

4.   Offering made by fire as sweet savor

C.   The peace offering (Leviticus 3)

1.   From the herd, male or female without blemish

2.   Killed at the door; its blood sprinkled on the altar

3.   Jesus is our peace; we have peace through His blood.

D.   The sin offering (Leviticus 4)

1.   For the sins of ignorance

2.   The priest needed a sacrifice for his own sins.

3.   All have sinned against God.

E.   The trespass offering (Leviticus 5)

1.   To remove the guilt of sin

2. The blood of the animal was sprinkled on the altar.

3. Man trespasses against man.

VIII. THE BRAZEN ALTAR IN REVELATION

A. Jesus as a Lamb that was slain (Revelation 5:6).

B. The angel cast fire of the altar into the earth (Revelation 8:5).

C. There is an altar in heaven (Revelation 11:1).

D. Another angel came out from the altar, which had power over fire (Revelation 14:18).

E. *And I heard another out of the altar say, Even so, Lord God Almighty, true and righteous are thy judgments* (Revelation 16:7).

THE FIRE OF GOD

THEME VERSES: EXODUS 13:21; 29:14,18

LOCATION: On the brazen altar and as a pillar of fire before the Israelites

OLD TESTAMENT SIGNIFICANCE: Consumed the sacrifice and led the way

POINTS TO JESUS: Jesus is our shelter and protection from the world. He is a consuming fire.

I Corinthians 3:13: *Every man's work shall be made manifest: for the day shall declare it, because it shall be revealed by fire; and the fire shall try every man's work of what sort it is.*

(Refer to Section I in this syllabus)

I. FIRE CAME FROM HEAVEN

A. The fire burned up the sacrifice in the most Holy Place.

1. The fire was sovereignly lit, but the priests were to keep it going.

      2.   Christ is our divine fire.

      3.   Christ will return with fire of vengeance (II Thessalonians 1:7-10).

  B. History of falling fire

      1.   Elijah built an altar (I Kings 18:38).

      2.   Fire consumed Job's sheep (Job 1:16).

      3.   God judged His people with fire (Isaiah 10:16-17).

      4.   God's anger brings judgment
          (Jeremiah 15:14; Lamentations 2:3).

      5.   Captivity and bondage are like a fire (Ezekiel 19).

      6.   Ungodly cities were judged (Genesis 19:24).

  C. Fire was taken from the brazen altar to the golden altar.

      1.   Fire fell at Pentecost.

      2.   We are to keep it going.

      3.   The fire on the sacrifice caused a sweet savor.

II. THE PILLAR OF FIRE LED THE ISRAELITES

  A. God's Presence

      1.   He guided them on their way to Canaan.

      2.   He was the light to their path.

  B. It protected them in the wilderness.

      1.   It kept them safe from their enemies.

      2.   The Cross of Jesus protects us from the world.

III. THE FIRE IN REVELATION

  A. Jesus' eyes are as fire (Revelation 1:14).

  B. The earth will be judged by fire (Revelation 18:8).

C. The devil, the beast, and the false prophet will be cast into the lake of fire (Revelation 20:10).

THE BRAZEN LAVER

THEME VERSES: EXODUS 30:17-21

LOCATION: Outer Court

OLD TESTAMENT SIGNIFICANCE: Priestly Purification

POINTS TO JESUS: He cleanses us from our sins.

Ephesians 5:26: *That he might sanctify and cleanse it with the washing of water by the word . . .*

(Refer to Section I, Chapter 2 in this syllabus)

I. **DESCRIPTION OF BRAZEN LAVER**

A. Made of brass

B. Women gave their mirrors for the brass (Exodus 38:8).

       1. Speaks of surrender

       2. Our mirror of what God has done

   C. No specific measurements

   D. Placed in Outer Court

   E. Purpose

       1. To cleanse from defilement

       2. For refreshment

       3. God used water to judge the world in Noah's flood.

II. BRASS HAS TO DO WITH JUDGMENT

   A. First the blood was shed at the brazen altar.

   B. Water was in the brazen laver.

III. THE PRIESTS WASHED IN THE BRAZEN LAVER

   A. Water of regeneration

   B. Water in baptism

   C. Three witnesses

IV. THE LAVER IN TRANSIT

   A. There were no staves to carry it.

   B. It was not to be covered when carried.

V. HISTORY OF THE LAVER

   A. Water was for cleansing.

       1. In Eden there was water to water the garden.

       2. Pharaoh and his hosts were drowned in water.

       3. It preserved the life of Hagar and her son.

       4. Water came out of a smitten rock.

5. It brought healing to Naaman.

6. It was important in the ministries of Elijah and Elisha.

B. The blood was a symbol of death and had to be washed away.

   1. We are dead in our sins and trespasses.

   2. We are cleansed by the washing of the water of the Word.

VI. THE BRAZEN LAVER IN REVELATION

A. Jesus is our fountain of life (Revelation 21:6).

B. The Spirit wants us to drink the water of life freely (Revelation 22:17).

THE DOOR

THEME VERSES: EXODUS 26:36-37

LOCATION: Across the whole length of the Tabernacle facing east; entrance to the Holy Place

OLD TESTAMENT SIGNIFICANCE: Entrance only for the priest

POINTS TO JESUS: Jesus is King, Son of Man, Son of God, and the Passover Lamb.

John 10:7: *Then said Jesus unto them again, Verily, verily, I say unto you, I am the door of the sheep.*

Outline

(Refer to Section I, Chapter 1 in this syllabus)

I. **MATERIALS**

    A. Blue, purple, and scarlet (divers colors) fine twined linen

    B. Wrought with needlework

II. **ENTRANCE**

    A. To the Holy Place

    B. Let the priests in but kept the Israelites out

    C. Covered by the veil

III. **GATES IN THE BIBLE**

    A. We are to possess the gates of our enemies.

    B. There is a gate in heaven.

    C. We are to enter in at the straight gate (Matthew 7:13-14).

    D. Suffering happened outside the gate.

    E. The gates of hell shall not prevail against the church.

    F. There are twelve gates of the heavenly city.

IV. **THE COLORS SIGNIFY JESUS CHRIST**

    A. Blue—Christ is the heavenly Son of God.

    B. Scarlet—Jesus is the Son of Man.

        1. Savior of mankind

        2. Left His heavenly home to tabernacle with man

3. Is now seated at the right hand of God the Father in heaven

C. Purple refers to Christ's Kingship

D. Blending red and blue makes purple.

   1. Jesus showed His kingship over death.

      a. Raised Jairus' daughter from the dead

      b. Called Lazarus forth from the grave

   2. Jesus operated in the natural realm as the Son of Man.

      a. Told them to feed the girl

      b. Told them to unwrap Lazarus from the death clothes

V. MEANING OF THE DOOR

A. Our praises are acceptable to Jesus.

B. We enter in with Him without judgment.

VI. PILLARS

A. There were five pillars of gold in the Tabernacle.

   1. The pillars were set in sockets of brass.

   2. Five is the number of grace.

B. Note the five pillars in the Bible.

   1. There are five books of the Pentateuch.

   2. James, Cephas (Peter), John, Barnabas, and Paul were referred to as pillars (Galatians 2:9).

   3. Five names of Christ (Isaiah 9:6)

      a. Wonderful

      b. Counsellor

      c. Mighty God

       d.   Everlasting Father

       e.   Prince of Peace

       f.   Fivefold ministries

VII. CHAPITERS AND SOCKETS

  A. Made of gold and brass

  B. Jesus endured the cross for the glory beyond.

VIII. THE PASSOVER

  A. Both judgment and mercy are found here (Exodus 12:27; Hebrews 11:28).

     1. Judgment came upon the firstborn of the Egyptians.

     2. Mercy was found behind the doors marked with the blood of the lamb.

  B. It became the beginning of months for Israel.

  C. The lamb was hidden fourteen days (Exodus 12:3-6).

     1. The first born was given to God (Exodus 13:11-13).

     2. A male—by man sin entered the world (Romans 5:12).

     3. Without spot or blemish (Exodus 12:5)

     4. The blood was applied to the door for deliverance (Exodus 12:7, 13, 22).

       a. Applied in three places

       b. Applied with hyssop

     5. The lamb was to be eaten inside the door.

       a. The head (mind)

       b. The legs (walk)

       c. The liver, heart, lungs (inward attitude)

6. Safety was found only inside the house.

7. The Passover shows the difference between God's people and the Egyptians.

8. The Passover brought the spoiling of the Egyptians

9. None were feeble or sick.

10. Exodus brought a song (Revelation 5:9-10; John 1:29, 36).

IX. THE DOOR IN REVELATION

A. The door of heaven is open for us (Revelation 3:8, 20).

1. No one can shut us off from God.

2. Salvation is a free gift from God.

B. God shows us things to come (Revelation 4:1).

C. There are three gates on each side of the heavenly city (Revelation 21:13).

THE HOLY PLACE

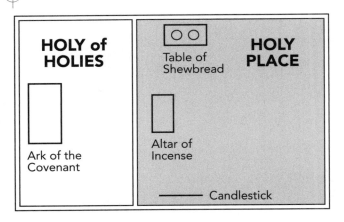

THEME VERSE: EXODUS 26:33

LOCATION: Between the outer court and the Holy of Holies

OLD TESTAMENT SIGNIFICANCE: Room of service and fellowship

POINTS TO JESUS: Jesus is holy and fills us with life and light and praise

I Peter 2:9, *But ye are a chose generation, a royal priesthood, an holy nation, a peculiar people; that ye should shew forth the praises of him who hath called you out of darkness into his marvellous light;*

I. **FILLED WITH THE TABLE OF SHEWBREWAD, THE CANDLESTICK, AND THE ALTAR OF INCENSE**

   A. The priests had provisions of bread.

      1. Fed the body

      2. Communion

   B. The light was provided for ministering to the Lord.

      1. There was no natural light in the Holy Place.

      2. The Word is the light in our life.

   C. The incense (prayers) led the way into the Holy of Holies.

      1. Service to God

      2. Closer walk with God

II. **PLACE OF HOLINESS**

   A. Symbol of the full ministry of Christ

   B. The glory of God filled the Holy Place.

   C. The power of the Holy Spirit was present.

III. **THE HOLY PLACE IN REVELATION**

   A. God is surrounded by praises in heaven (Revelation 4:8).

   B. Believers are holy people (Revelation 22:11).

TABLE OF SHEWBREAD

THEME VERSES: EXODUS 25:23-30

LOCATION: The Holy Place on the north side

OLD TESTAMENT SIGNIFICANCE: Provision for the priests

POINTS TO JESUS: Jesus is the Bread of Life.

John 6:51, *I am the living bread which came down from heaven: if any man eat of this bread, he shall live for ever: and the bread that I will give is my flesh, which I will give for the life of the world.*

I. **DESCRIPTION OF THE TABLE**

    A. Shittim wood

    B. Dimensions of the table

        1. Two cubit length

    2. A cubit breadth

    3. A cubit and a half height

  C. Overlaid with gold

  D. Surrounded with crown

  E. Staves of wood covered with gold

II. VESSELS ON THE TABLE

  A. Three types

    1. Dishes to hold the food-bread

    2. Spoons of hollow gold with incense

    3. Bowls and covers for the wine

  B. The Shewbread

    1. Its names

      a. Bread of Presence

      b. Bread of Faces

      c. Bread of Order or Arrangement

    2. It was placed on the north side of the Holy Place.

    3. Sprinkled with frankincense

      a. We eat at His table in the Light of His Presence.

      b. Incense is a prayer of worship and adoration.

    4. Aaron's sons ate the bread.

III. THE TABLE IN TRANSIT

  A. Covered by a blue cloth

    1. A representation of the Holy Spirit

    2. The color of heaven and Christ as the Lord from heaven

B. The dishes, spoons, bowls, and covering of scarlet.

    1. Blood sacrifice

    2. Jesus is the Sacrificial One

C. Badgers' skins were the final covering.

    1. God is over all.

    2. There is no natural beauty in unregenerate man.

IV. THE TABLE IN SOLOMON'S TEMPLE

A. The singers at Solomon's table

    1. Ten tables with 120 loaves of bread

    2. The church is the fullness of God with the power of the Holy Spirit.

    3. Song and singing were always connected with the table of the Lord (Mark 14:26).

V. HISTORY OF THE BREAD

A. Unleavened bread was used at Passover (Exodus 12:14-20, 34).

B. Manna

    1. Nourished Israel for 40 years in the wilderness (Exodus 16)

    2. The Ark of the Covenant contained the golden pot of manna (Hebrews 9:4).

C. Offerings

    1. The meal offering of fine flour was a type of bread (Leviticus 2).

    2. Bread was used at Pentecost in the two wave loaves (Leviticus 23:17).

    3. Abraham gave bread to the Lord (Genesis 18:1-6).

    4. Abraham received bread and wine from Melchizedek (Genesis 14:18).

D. Physical

1. Elijah went 40 days on the strength of the bread and water that the angel brought to him (I Kings 19:8).

2. David received strength from the shewbread (I Samuel 21:6).

3. Mephibosheth sat at the king's table as a son (II Samuel 9:7-13).

E. Restoration

1. Hezekiah restores the order of the table under his reformation (II Chronicles 29:18).

2. The shewbread is restored again after the Babylonian captivity under Nehemiah   (Nehemiah 10:33).

3. During our communion remembrance, we eat "raised bread" which symbolized the resurrection power available to us today.

F. Miracles

1. Jesus fed 5,000 people with five loaves and two fishes (Matthew 14:15-21).

2. 4,000 people were fed with miracle bread and fishes (Matthew 15:32-38).

VI. BREAD IN REVELATION

A. Overcomers will eat of the tree of life (Revelation 2:7).

B. Overcomers will eat of the hidden manna (Revelation 2:17).

GOLDEN CANDLESTICK

THEME VERSES: EXODUS 25:31-33

See also: Psalms 18:28

LOCATION: The Holy Place on the south side

OLD TESTAMENT SIGNIFICANCE: Provided light for the priests to minister in the Holy Place

POINTS TO JESUS: Jesus is the light of the world, *. . . the true Light, which lighteth every man that cometh into the world* (John 1:9).

The candlestick was from a solid block of gold, beaten into its beautiful form. Jesus was the pure (gold), sinless sacrifice, bruised and beaten for us.

Outline

(Refer to Section I, Chapter 4 of this syllabus)

I. **THE GOLDEN CANDLESTICK BROUGHT ABOUT ILLUMINATION INTO THE HOLY PLACE**

    A. Description of the candlestick

1. One piece of gold

2. Single shaft with many extending branches

   a. Knop

   b. Flower

   c. Almond bowl

3. Lamps, not candles

4. Light from the Brazen Altar

   a. Pure olive oil

II. THE LAMP WAS LIT IN THE EVENING

A. Illuminated the Holy Place

   1. Symbolic of the Holy Spirit illuminating our spiritual understanding to the things of God

III. THE CANDLESTICK IN TRANSIT

A. Cloth of blue

B. Badger's skin

C. Carried on a bar

IV. CANDLESTICK IN SOLOMON'S TEMPLE

A. Ten golden candlesticks

B. Candlesticks of silver in the priest's chambers

C. Candlesticks in Babylon (Daniel 5:1-5)

V. CANDLESTICKS IN THE BOOK OF REVELATION

A. Candlesticks symbolize churches (Revelation 2-4).

   1. Churches carry the light of the Gospel to the world.

B. The candlestick has seven branches.

1. The seven branches represent the seven Spirits of God.

2. The Lamb has seven eyes which are the seven Spirits of God (Revelation 5:6).

C. The two olive trees and the two candlesticks symbolize the two witnesses (Revelation 11:4; Zechariah 4:11-14).

GOLDEN ALTAR OF INCENSE

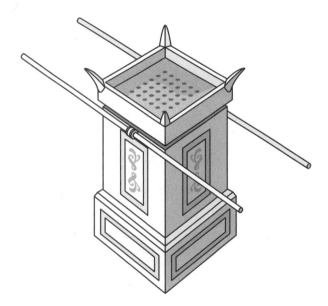

THEME VERSES: EXODUS 31:1-9

See also Psalms 141:2

LOCATION: The Holy Place on the west side

OLD TESTAMENT SIGNIFICANCE: Used to burn perpetual incense unto the Lord; the priest prayed for the people at this altar.

POINTS TO JESUS: The golden altar foreshadowed Jesus, our High Priest, Who intercedes to the Father on our behalf (Romans 8:34; Hebrews 7:25) and Who presents our praises to the Father (Hebrews 13:15; I Peter 2:5).

Outline

(Refer to Section I, Chapter 2 in this syllabus)

IX. THE DESCRIPTION OF THE GOLDEN ALTAR OF INCENSE

    A. Made of shittim wood covered with gold

    B. It was the tallest and the smallest piece of Tabernacle furniture.

    C. It had four horns, one in each corner (Revelation 9:13).

        1. A horn is symbolic of power in Scripture.

            a. There is a tremendous power in prayer and praise.

    D. The altar had a crown of gold.

        1. Represented the sinless, risen Conqueror

    E. It had two gold rings for transport.

    F. It was placed immediately in front of the veil in the Holy Place.

II. THE PURPOSE OF THE GOLDEN ALTAR OF INCENSE

    A. To burn incense

        1. Incense is symbolic of prayer.

        2. Incense is described as sweet, pure, holy, and perpetual.

            a. This describes Jesus' prayers for us.

        3. Coals used only from brazen altar

    B. Placed where the priest offered up prayers for the people

        1. He burned incense morning and night

    C. Once a year, blood was put in the horns.

III. HISTORY OF THE GOLDEN ALTAR

    A. Korah (Numbers 16:1-35)

1. Led 250 men in rebellion against God and Moses in the wilderness

2. Offered incense and "strange fire" unto the Lord

3. The earth opened up and swallowed them.

B. Nadab and Abihu, sons of Aaron (Leviticus 10:1-2)

   1. Offered incense and "strange fire" to the Lord

   2. Consumed by fire from the Lord

C. Uzziah (II Chronicles 26:16-21)

   1. Transgressed against the Lord

   2. Burnt incense at the golden altar

   3. Smitten with leprosy while still in the Temple

D. Zacharias (Luke 1:5-11)

   1. Had visitation from an angel while praying at altar of incense

   2. The angel told him he would have a son to be named, John.

   3. Because of his unbelief, Zacharias had his ability to speak taken from him until the birth of his son.

IV. JESUS IS OUR INTERCESSOR

A. Even now, He is at the right hand of God, interceding for us (Romans 8:34).

   1. Like the incense, His prayers are sweet, pure, holy, and perpetual.

   2. Like the altar, Jesus is crowned (with glory and honor).

B. Jesus presents our praises to the Father

   1. By Him, we offer the sacrifice of praise to God continually (Hebrews 13:15).

V. THE GOLDEN ALTAR OF INCENSE IN REVELATION

  A. Opening of the seventh seal (Revelation 8:3-4)

   1. An angel offers incense along with the prayers of the saints at the altar.

     a. Incense and prayers ascend to God.

  B. Sixth angel with trumpet (Revelation 9:13-14)

   1. Voice from altar looses angels from Euphrates River

THE VEIL

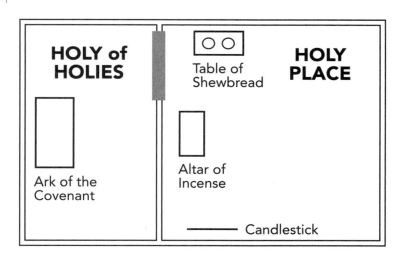

THEME VERSES: EXODUS 26:31-33

LOCATION: Between Holy Place and Holy of Holies

OLD TESTAMENT SIGNIFICANCE: Divided the Holy Place from the Holy of Holies; kept the glory of God contained in the Holy of Holies as a protection for sinful man who would die in the presence of God.

POINTS TO JESUS: The veil is a type of Jesus' flesh (Hebrews 10:19-20).

(Refer to Section I, Chapter 1 in this syllabus)

I. DESCRIPTION OF THE VEIL

A. Fine-twined linen

1. White symbolized Jesus' purity

2. Blue symbolized Jesus' divinity

3. Red expresses Jesus' humanity

4. Purple, as a combination of red and blue, illustrated the fact that Jesus was both man and God.

B. Images of cherubim were woven into the veil.

1. Reminder of cherubim posted outside of Garden of Eden (Genesis 3:24)

C. Hung on four pillars of wood, covered with gold

1. Wood symbolized Jesus as a man.

2. Gold symbolized Jesus as God.

D. Suspended by gold hooks with silver sockets

II. DIFFERENT VEILS IN SCRIPTURE

A. Veil of the Tabernacle

B. Veil of Solomon's Temple (II Chronicles 3:14)

C. The veil of Moses (Exodus 34:33-35)

D. The veil of Christ's flesh (Hebrews 10:19-20)

E. The veil of unbelief (II Corinthians 3:13-16)

F. The veil of national blindness (Isaiah 25:7-9)

III. JESUS AND THE VEIL IN THE TABERNACLE

    A.   The veil split in two at the crucifixion (Matthew 27:51).

        1.   Split from the top to the bottom

            a.   Jesus, as God, opened the way for man to have open access to God.

        2.   Foreshadows Jesus' triumphant return to the Mount of Olives when the mountain will be rent in two (Zechariah 14:4)

    B.   Jesus passed through the veil in the heavenly Temple when He presented His blood to the Father for our sin (Hebrews 6:9; 9).

        1.   The veil we go through to access God now is Jesus' flesh (Hebrews 10:19-20).

    C.   There is a veil over the mind of the Jews until they receive Christ as their Messiah (II Corinthians 3:13-16).

THE HOLY OF HOLIES

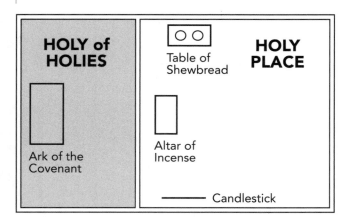

THEME VERSES: EXODUS 26:33-34

LOCATION: Inside the Holy Place, set apart by the veil

OLD TESTAMENT SIGNIFICANCE: The place exclusively set apart for the Presence of God

POINTS TO JESUS: The Holy of Holies represented God meeting or communing with man. Through Jesus, the union of God with man was perfected.

Outline

(Refer to Section I, Chapter 1 in this syllabus)

I. **DESCRIPTION OF THE HOLY OF HOLIES**

   A. Section in the Holy Place partitioned off by the veil

   B. Lit by the glory of God

      1. No natural or artificial light used

   C. Contained only the Ark of the Covenant and the mercy seat

   D. Entered once a year

      1. On the Day of Atonement, the high priest entered to acquire forgiveness for the sins of the nation.

II. **HISTORY OF THE HOLY OF HOLIES**

   A. God established the Holy of Holies as the place where His presence would reside.

   B. When the Ark was placed in the Holy of Holies, the glory cloud filled the Temple (I Kings 8:6-10).

III. **JESUS AND THE HOLY OF HOLIES**

   A. Jesus took His blood into the heavenly Holy of Holies (Hebrews 9:3-14).

      1. By presenting His blood He bridged the chasm between a holy God and sinful man.

      2. Now man has free access to communion with God (Hebrews 4:16).

IV. THE HOLY OF HOLIES IN THE END TIMES

    A. The Antichrist will sit on a throne in the Holy of Holies (Matthew 24:15).

ARK OF THE COVENANT

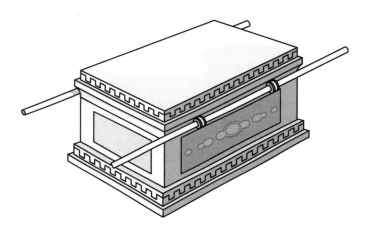

THEME VERSES: EXODUS 25:10-16

LOCATION: Holy of Holies

OLD TESTAMENT SIGNIFICANCE: Symbolized God's presence among His people, and how His Covenant blessing rested upon them

POINTS TO JESUS: Jesus is our Ark of the Covenant. In Him is the full presence of God, the fulfillment of the Law, our victory.

Outline

(Refer to Section I, Chapter 2 in this syllabus)

I.   DESCRIPTION OF THE ARK OF THE COVENANT

    A. Made of shittim wood covered with gold

B. Two and one half cubits long, one and a half cubits high

C. Crown of gold encircles the top

D. Four gold rings were mounted on the sides for carrying the Ark.

II. THE CONTENTS OF THE ARK

A. The two stone tablets

1. Ten Commandments written by the finger of God

B. Aaron's rod that budded (Numbers 16,17)

1. Symbol of God's delivering power

2. Confirmed Aaron's line as God's choice for the priesthood

C. Gold pot of manna

1. Represented God's complete provision for His people

D. Copy of the Pentateuch (Book of the Law)

1. Recorded history of God's dealings with His people

III. HISTORY OF THE ARK

A. In the wilderness

1. The Ark gave the Israelites direction because the cloud of God's presence hovered over the Ark (Numbers 10:33-36).

B. Entering the Promised Land

1. Crossing the Jordan (Joshua 3:5-17)

   a. Priests carried the Ark into the Jordan River.

   b. The Jordan waters separated.

   c. The Israelites walked across dry ground.

2. The Ark led the march around Jericho (Joshua 6:1-20).

C. Led the Israelites to victory in many battles.

D. Captured by the Philistines (I Samuel 4,5)

E. Returned to Israel (I Samuel 6; II Samuel 6)

IV. JESUS IS OUR ARK

A. He is the embodiment of the presence of God (Colossians 2:9).

B. In Him, we have all provision (Philippians 4:19).

C. He is our deliverer (Galatians 1:4; Hebrews 2:14-15).

D. He fulfilled the Law (Matthew 5:17).

E. He guides us by His Holy Spirit (John 16:13).

V. JESUS IS OUR HIGH PRIEST

A. Jesus sprinkled His blood on the heavenly Ark (Hebrews 9).

VI. THE ARK OF THE COVENANT IN REVELATION

A. At the third woe, the Temple in heaven is opened and the Ark is visible (Revelation 11:19).

THE MERCY SEAT

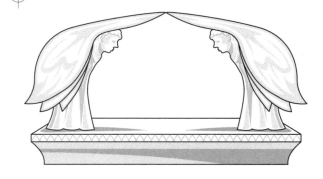

THEME VERSES: EXODUS 25:17-22

LOCATION: The Holy of Holies, above the Ark of the Covenant, beneath the cherubim

OLD TESTAMENT SIGNIFICANCE: Once a year, the High Priest entered the Holy of Holies where he made atonement for the sins of Israel by sprinkling blood on the mercy seat.

The mercy seat formed God's throne on earth: *And Hezekiah prayed before the LORD, and said, O LORD God of Israel, which dwellest between the cherubims . . .* (II Kings 19:15).

POINTS TO JESUS: The same Greek word for *mercy seat* is also translated *propitiation* and means "to appease, to placate, to make satisfactory." Jesus made propitiation for us at the cross. He took the punishment for our sins so that we might obtain mercy instead of the judgment we deserved (see Romans 3:24-25).

(Refer to Section I, Chapter 2 of this syllabus)

I. **THE MERCY SEAT WAS THE THRONE OF GOD'S MERCY FOR THE ISRAELITES**

   A. Description of the mercy seat

      1. Made from a solid sheet of pure gold

         a. Most valuable of all the Tabernacle furniture.

      2. Two cherubim stood on either end of the mercy seat, with wings outstretched over it.

         a. They are symbolically protecting God's throne.

         b. Cherubim are found in the Word in connection with God's judgment, but over the mercy seat, they had to do with mercy.

         c. Cherubim are the highest of the angelic order (Revelation 5:11-14).

      3. The mercy seat served as a lid to the Ark of the Covenant.

         a. The same size as the Ark in length and breadth

      b. Completely covered the Ten Commandments

      c. God's mercy covers His people's sin when the blood is applied.

B. The mercy seat was the place where God met the sinner in the person of His representative.

  1. The high priest sprinkled blood seven times once a year on the mercy seat.

  2. The blood cried mercy.

C. The mercy seat was the place of communion where man actually met God.

  1. God spoke to Moses from the mercy seat (Numbers 7:89).

  2. God spoke to the high priest from the mercy seat.

D. The mercy seat shows that God would find His rest in the final work of Christ.

E. Isaiah had a vision of the throne in heaven from which the mercy seat was patterned (Isaiah 6:1-3).

II. JESUS AND THE MERCY SEAT

A. After completing the work of redemption, Jesus sat down on the mercy seat in the heavenly Temple (Hebrews 10:11-12).

B. Jesus sprinkled His blood on the heavenly mercy seat (Hebrews 10:19-22).

  1. Now we have access to the throne to receive mercy (Hebrews 4:16).

III. THE THRONE, SYMBOLIZED BY THE MERCY SEAT, IN THE BOOK OF REVELATION:

A. *After this I beheld, and, lo, a great multitude, which no man could number, of all nations, and kindreds, and people, and tongues, stood before the throne, and before the Lamb, clothed with white robes, and palms in their hands; And cried with a loud voice, saying, Salvation to our God which sitteth upon the throne,*

and unto the Lamb. And all the angels stood round about the throne, and about the elders and the four beasts, and fell before the throne on their faces, and worshipped God, . . .
(Revelation 7:9-11).

THE GLORY CLOUD

THEME VERSES: EXODUS 40:34-38

See also Exodus 24:15-18

LOCATION: In the Tabernacle: the cloud hovered over the mercy seat between the cherubim in the Holy of Holies.

In the wilderness: the cloud served as the beacon or guide to lead them.

OLD TESTAMENT SIGNIFICANCE: God inhabited the glory cloud. When the cloud descended into the Tabernacle, it was the first time God Himself dwelt in the midst of sinful man.

POINTS TO JESUS: Jesus was the embodiment of the presence and glory of God. *The Word became flesh and made his dwelling among us. We have seen his glory, the glory of the One and Only, who came from the Father, full of grace and truth* (John 1:14 NIV).

The cloud was to Israel what the Holy Spirit is to the church today, a leader and a guide.

(Refer to Section I, Chapter 2 of this syllabus)

I. THE CLOUD OF GLORY

II. THE CLOUD BROUGHT BLESSINGS (Exodus 13:21-22)

    A. The cloud gave them direction.

        1. It went before them.

2. It led them.

3. It gave them a light in the darkness.

4. It gave them warmth.

5. It was a shade from the heat of the day.

III. THE CLOUD IN THE WILDERNESS

A. First appeared as the Hebrews left Egypt en route to the Red Sea (Exodus 13:21)

B. The cloud led the Hebrews through the Red Sea (I Corinthians 10:1-2).

   1. Shielded the Hebrew camp from the Egyptian army prior to crossing the Red Sea (Exodus 14:19-20)

   2. Troubled the Egyptian host in the Red Sea (Exodus 14:24)

C. The glory appeared in the cloud (Exodus 16:10).

D. The cloud brought Israel to Sinai and settled on the Mount (Exodus 19:9-19).

E. Moses went into the cloud on Mt. Sinai for forty days and nights and received the Ten Commandments from God (Exodus 24:15-18; 34:5-7).

F. At the dedication of the Tabernacle, the cloud moved into the Holy of Holies (Exodus 40:34-38).

G. The cloud governed all the journeying of Israel in the wilderness, finally leading them to the Promised Land.

IV. THE CLOUD IN LATER OLD TESTAMENT HISTORY

A. The cloud moved into Solomon's Temple at its dedication (I Kings 8:10-11).

B. Isaiah prophesied that the cloud would bring revival to Egypt (Isaiah 19:1).

C. Ezekiel saw the cloud in his visions of heaven and the glory of God (Ezekiel 8:11; 10:3, 4).

D. Daniel saw a vision of Jesus returning to earth on the cloud (Daniel 7:13-14).

E. The tragic end of the history of the cloud as seen in the Old Testament occurred when the glory cloud eventually departed from the Temple (Ezekiel 10:1-22).

V. JESUS AND THE CLOUD

A. In the Gospels

1. Mount of Transfiguration (Matthew 17:5)

2. Jesus' Ascension back to the Father (Acts 1:9)

B. In the end times

1. Jesus is clothed with a cloud (Revelation 10:1).

2. Jesus is seated upon a white cloud (Revelation 14:14-16).

3. He will return to earth in a cloud of glory (Luke 21:27).

4. He will also come in clouds of glory with His saints (Mark 14:62; Matthew 26:64; I Thessalonians 4:17; Hebrews 12:1).

5. The glory that was in the cloud will be the eternal joy of the redeemed in the City of God, the New Jerusalem.

THE CROSS

THEME VERSES: Ephesians 2:12-16

OLD TESTAMENT SIGNIFICANCE: The Tabernacle looked forward to the cross.

POINTS TO JESUS: Jesus made the ultimate sacrifice for the sin of mankind through His death on the cross.

Outline

I. **THE TABERNACLE FORESHADOWED JESUS ON THE CROSS**

   A. Brazen Altar—Jesus was the Lamb slain for us (I Peter 1:19; Revelation 13:8).

   B. Laver—Jesus was the Lamb without sin (John 1:29).

   C. Candlestick—Jesus' sacrifice brings light to all who receive Him (John 1:4-5).

   D. Table of Shewbread—Jesus is the Bread of Life Who gave His life that we might live (John 6:33-35).

   E. Altar of Incense—Jesus' atoning work on the cross gave us access to God in prayer and praise (Hebrews 4:16).

   F. Ark of the Covenant—on the cross, Jesus cut a new covenant with God (Hebrews 8:6-13).

   G. Mercy Seat—the cross is the greatest illustration of God's mercy in the history of mankind (Ephesians 2:4).

II. **THE FIVE WOUNDS OF CHRIST AND THE FIVE "I WILLS" OF SATAN**

   A. Jesus was wounded in five places:

      1. Head, forced to wear a crown of thorns

      2. Back, whipped

      3. Hands, pierced by nails

      4. Feet, pierced by nails

      5. Side, wounded by sword

   B. Satan's five "I wills" (Isaiah 14:12-14)

      1. I will ascend into heaven.

      2. I will exalt my throne above the stars of God.

      3. I will sit also upon the mount of the congregation, in the sides of the north.

4. I will ascend above the heights of the clouds.

5. I will be like the most High.

III. WE HAVE AN ALTAR (HEBREWS 13:10)

A. Every person needs an altar.

B. Judgment begins at the altar (I Peter 4:17).

IV. JESUS IS OUR MEDIATOR

A. A mediator is one who reconciles opposing parties.

1. Man was separated from God by sin (Romans 3:23).

2. Jesus reconciled us to God (I Timothy 2:5).

B. A mediator is one who chooses to undertake the work of making peace.

1. Jesus obtained peace for us on the cross (Colossians 1:20).

C. A mediator seeks the greater good at the cost of his own pleasure.

1. Jesus chose God's will over His own (Luke 22:42).

D. A mediator has a servant attitude in accomplishing his work.

1. Jesus took on the form of a servant (Philippians 2:7).

2. Jesus was meek and lowly in heart (Matthew 11:29).

E. A mediator is made sole judge in the matter.

1. God committed all judgment to the Son (John 5:26-27).

V. BY THE CROSS

A. We are reconciled to God (Romans 5:10).

1. We have access to God (Hebrews 10:19-22).

2. We gain Righteousness (II Corinthians 5:21).

B. We are saved from God's wrath (Romans 5:9).

C. We receive atonement (Romans 5:11).

D. We are given peace (Colossians 1:20).

  1. We can receive a clean conscience (Hebrews 10:22).

E. Our nation can succeed in racial reconciliation (Ephesians 2:16-18).

F. We have authority in the name of Jesus (Philippians 2:9-11; Mark 16:17-18).

G. We have the power of God (Ephesians 1:19-20).

Pray through the Tabernacle

As we come to the end of Section II, we begin to see how the symbolism of the Tabernacle relates to us today. We marvel that ages ago, God put in motion a plan to help us know Him personally in all His peace, righteousness, authority, and power. The way to receive all these advantages is to invite Jesus Christ into your life as your Savior. If you would like to make today the day of power, change, and blessing in your life, pray this prayer:

O God, I am a sinner. I realize that Jesus was sacrificed on the cross to take away my sin and give me open access to You; in doing so, He fulfilled the plan you outlined in the tabernacle ages ago.

I want to turn from sin and receive Jesus Christ as my Savior. I believe in my heart You raised Jesus from the dead, and I confess Him as my Lord. From this moment on, I will follow Him and serve You.

Finally, Father, I ask you to fill me with Your Holy Spirit.

In Jesus' Name I pray,

Amen

Notes

Notes

Notes

THE TABERNACLE
SYLLABUS

Section 3
DEVOTIONS:
PRAYING THROUGH THE TABERNACLE

Contents

Introduction

PRAYING THROUGH THE TABERNACLE

Now that we have thoroughly studied each piece of the Tabernacle furniture and understand the significance of each, it is time to pray through the Tabernacle. As New Covenant priests, we have access to every part of God's Tabernacle, so we can boldly walk through the Tabernacle—by faith —and appropriate the symbolism of each piece of furniture into our own prayer lives.

The following pages will both give you a good example of *how* to meditate on the significance of the Tabernacle and provide you with a sample prayer you may use in your private time with the Lord.

You will see I've given plenty of space for you, so you can compose your own prayers, record revelations God gives you as you pray, and/or write down the answers you receive from spending time with Him.

As you devote some quality time to praying through the Tabernacle, I am confident you will have some special encounters with the Holy Spirit, Jesus will become more real to you, and your intimate fellowship with our Father will grow.

> *The grace of the Lord Jesus Christ, and the love of God, and the communion of the Holy Ghost, be with you all. Amen* (II Corinthians 13:14).

PRAYING THROUGH THE BRAZEN ALTAR

Upon entering the Tabernacle's Outer Court, one is immediately confronted by the brazen altar. On the altar, sacrifice is made to atone for sin and to appease God's justice, righteousness, and holiness.

Not only are we struck by the enormity of the altar (7½ feet by 4½ feet) but we are impressed by the amount of blood covering and surrounding the altar.

BODY: Animals without fault or blemish were presented to the priests as a sacrifice for the people. The Law exacted penalties and punishments for transgressing the law. Every sin required a sacrifice —the death of a living animal—so the transgressor of the Law would not be required to forfeit his own life.

The people saw the altar and the priestly rituals prior to the sacrifice. They brought the sacrificial animals, choosing the best of their flocks or herds. They smelled the animal's burning flesh on the altar and saw it consumed by fire. They were allowed limited participation, but without first presenting a sacrificial animal before God, the Israelites could proceed no further in their relationship with God. Sacrifice *had* to be made.

SOUL: Moses explained why sacrifices had to be made—sin separated man from God. No one bearing the slightest taint of sin —whether an outwardly visible or generally hidden defect—could approach God. Intercession made on their behalf by God's appointed emissaries, the priests, was their only means of reaching Him.

Relationship based on sacrifice was the only thing the people knew. If they obeyed the formulas given to Moses on Mount Sinai, they could expect God's blessing and favor; otherwise, they would suffer the consequences of disobedience. To them, atonement meant they escaped God's disfavor and would instead be blessed, for their obedience.

SPIRIT: Despite the significance of sacrifices on the brazen altar— an animal life forfeited in place of a human life as atonement for disobedience to the holy Law of God—there were deeper implications beyond the outward rite. Could the sacrifices made at the brazen altar bring an inner change in the person bringing the sacrifice? NO! The sacrifice was insufficient to make them holy and righteous before God. Did that mean then, the sacrifice held something inherent that by merely presenting it to the priest to be sacrificed ensured forgiveness of sins? NO! Forgiveness of sins was assured by the relationship between God and the person bringing the sacrifice. The offering of the sacrifices by the people indicated to God they were obeying Him with a heart of love and adoration.

Little did most of the Israelites know, in the slaying of thousands of animals on the brazen altar, there was deep symbolism of an ultimate sacrifice to come in the future, a sacrifice of a perfect and holy Lamb, the Messiah.

Five separate sacrifices portrayed the sufficiency of Christ's vicarious death on the Cross.

1. The *sin offering* represents forgiveness for the sins we commit against God.

   One of the first declarations made about Jesus was . . . *thou shalt call his name JESUS: for he shall save his people from their sins* (Matthew 1:21).

   This was prophesied by Gabriel prior to Jesus' birth. Throughout the Gospels numerous remarks were made to His being the means by which Israel's sins would be forgiven. Just before the beginning of Jesus' ministry, John the Baptist declared, *Behold the Lamb of God, which taketh away the sin of the world* (see John 1:29). To the Jews, equating Jesus to the Passover lamb could signal only one thing—the promised Messiah had come. During Jesus' life on earth He performed miracles; many times these miracles were preceded or followed by the forgiveness of sins or a display of mercy (e.g., Matthew 9:2-8; Luke 5:18-26; John 8:1-11). Jesus' sacrifice on the Cross was effective in removing the sin separating man from God.

2. The *trespass offering* signifies forgiveness of sins committed against others.

   All humans bear the guilt of Adam's transgression. Not only have we offended God, but we have damaged our relationships with others. We have a tendency to be self-centered, putting our own desires and wishes above those of others. Paul asserts that:

*. . . God was in Christ, reconciling the world unto himself,
not imputing their trespasses unto them; and hath committed
unto us the word of reconciliation . . . For he hath made him
to be sin for us, who knew no sin; that we might be made
the righteousness of God in him* (II Corinthians 5:19,21).

God has made a way for us to be reconciled to Him and for us
to be reconciled to one another. Offense and injury to us are not
easily forgotten or forgiven. However, because God has not dealt
with us according to our sins (see Psalms 103:8-14), we can offer
the same forgiveness to others since we are recipients of God's
love and forgiveness:

*Let all bitterness, and wrath, and anger, and clamour, and
evil speaking, be put away from you, with all malice: And
be ye kind one to another, tenderhearted, forgiving one
another, even as God for Christ's sake hath forgiven you*
(Ephesians 4:31-32).

3. The *burnt offering* points to the way the blood consecrates and
   dedicates us to God.

   The demands that are made on us to meet God's standards
   seem utterly impossible to attain. He requires we be holy even
   as He is holy (see I Peter 1:15). We are to be free from sin to enter
   into His holy hill (see Psalms 24:3-4). In heaven there will be nothing
   that defiles—no liars, sorcerers, whoremongers, murderers, or idola-
   ters (see Revelation 21:8; 22:15). So how is it possible to please
   God? As we have seen in the two previous items, it is through the
   work of Christ. Likewise, we are sanctified, set apart to serve God,
   through the operation of the Holy Spirit given to believers by the
   Lord Jesus after He ascended into heaven. The Spirit enables us
   by divine *dunamis*—**power**—to live a life pleasing to God.

   *I beseech you therefore, brethren, by the mercies of God,
   that ye present your bodies a living sacrifice, holy, acceptable
   unto God, which is your reasonable service. And be not con-
   formed to this world: but be ye transformed by the renewing
   of your mind, that ye may prove what is that good, and
   acceptable, and perfect, will of God* (Romans 12:1-2).

   Jesus promised that if we abide in Him, the Vine, we would
   draw our life from Him; and through His life we would be able

to live according to God's intention for us (John 15:1-4). Our consecration to God flows from the life He placed in us when we were born again. The mighty God, Who framed the worlds out of nothing, simply speaking them into being, this mighty God DWELLS in us—we have no excuse for being weak and ineffective. God *According as his divine power hath given unto us all things that pertain unto life and godliness, through the knowledge of him that hath called us to glory and virtue . . .* (II Peter 1:3). Tap into the inexhaustible source of power—live unto God, be transformed and transform your world through that power!

4. **The *peace offering*** expresses the peace available to us through Jesus' blood.

   At the fall, fellowship between the Creator and His creatures was severely limited. Man lost peace with God, the peace of God, and the peace between him and other men. God's initial intention was to have unbroken fellowship with the creature that most resembled Him. Here, in the person of man, was someone with whom God felt affinity—after all, man was in God's likeness.

   Yet when the serpent beguiled Eve, and Adam willfully disobeyed God's commandment not to eat of the tree of the knowledge of good and evil, humanity lost the ability to fully communicate with God. The peace offering solved the problem to a certain extent. When Jesus came with all His glorious, positive ramifications, peace once again became obtainable.

   Through Jesus' death, resurrection, and ascension, what was lost and damaged by the Fall has been restored. Once again, what satan meant for evil, God turned into eternal benefit to us by Jesus Christ. What has been restored?

   • God's peace *to* us—John 14:27

   • Peace *with* God—Romans 5:1

   • God *is* our peace—Ephesians 2:14

   • His peace makes possible peace *between* men —Ephesians 2:11-17

   • The peace *of* God—Philippians 4:7

- All this peace was accomplished through the blood of His cross
  —Colossians 1:20

Peace, peace, wonderful peace

Coming down from the Father above.

Sweep over my spirit, forever I pray,

In fathomless billows of love.

(*Wonderful Peace*, Cornell/Cooper, 1889)

5. The *meat offering* pictured the perfect sacrifice of Jesus' perfect humanity.

Leviticus 2 gives a brief description of the elements of the meat or meal offering. The composition of this offering consisted of flour (without leaven), oil, salt, and frankincense. What was the purpose of this offering?

It was *to be an offering made by fire, of a sweet savour unto the LORD* . . . (Leviticus 2:2).

The flour has been understood frequently to refer to the perfect humanity of Christ. Scripture clearly states Jesus was completely without sin:

For we have not an high priest which cannot be touched with the feeling of our infirmities; but was in all points tempted like as we are, yet without sin (Hebrews 4:15).

For such an high priest became us, who is holy, harmless, undefiled, separate from sinners, and made higher than the heavens . . . (Hebrews 7:26).

Leaven is a reference to sin in the Old and New Testaments. Jesus referred to the leaven of the Pharisees as being something negative (see Matthew 16:6,11). Paul, in I Corinthians, alludes to leaven as being synonymous with sin:

Purge out therefore the old leaven, that ye may be a new lump, as ye are unleavened. For even Christ our passover is sacrificed for us: Therefore let us keep the feast, not with old leaven, neither with the leaven of malice and wickedness; but with the unleavened bread of sincerity and truth (I Corinthians 5:7-8).

In the meal offering no leaven was to be found. It was devoid of any hint of impurity. Likewise, the flour was of the finest ground grains, sifted and beaten small. No imperfection or flaw could be found in the flour either. This perfectly describes the sinless humanity of Jesus Christ.

In the second chapter of Leviticus, there are many references to the oil and how it was to be used. In verse 1 the oil is *poured* upon the offering. In verse 4 the oil is *mingled* with the offering. In verse 7 the oil is to be offered *with* the meal sacrifice. Oil is used many times in the Bible as a picture of the Holy Spirit.

Jesus' life corresponds with the three uses of oil above. When Jesus was conceived, He was conceived by miraculous means which denotes the oil being *mingled* with the offering. Thus, He is called the Son of God:

And in the sixth month the angel Gabriel was sent from God unto a city of Galilee, named Nazareth, To a virgin espoused to a man whose name was Joseph, of the house of David; and the virgin's name was Mary. And the angel came in unto her, and said, Hail, thou that art highly favoured, the Lord is with thee: blessed art thou among women. And when she saw him, she was troubled at his saying, and cast in her mind what manner of salutation this should be. And the angel said unto her, Fear not, Mary: for thou hast found favour with God. And, behold, thou shalt conceive in thy womb, and bring forth a son, and shalt call his name JESUS. He shall be great, and shall be called the Son of the Highest: and the Lord God shall give unto him the throne of his father David: And he shall reign over the house of Jacob forever; and of his kingdom there shall be no end. Then said Mary unto the angel, How shall this be, seeing I know not a

*man? And the angel answered and said unto her, The
Holy Ghost shall come upon thee, and the power of
the Highest shall overshadow thee: therefore also that
holy thing which shall be born of thee shall be called
the Son of God* (Luke 1:26-35).

Prior to Jesus' public ministry, John the Baptist baptized
Him in the Jordan River. When He was baptized the Holy
Spirit descended on Him in the form of a dove (see Matthew
3:16). The meal offering was brought with the oil *poured*
on it. What a marvelous picture we have of this very thing
occurring when Jesus was baptized! The psalmist speaks of
the coming Messiah in Psalms 45:7, ***Thou lovest righteousness,
and hatest wickedness: therefore God, thy God, hath anointed
thee with the oil of gladness above thy fellows.*** Jesus spoke of
Himself as being anointed with the Spirit when He read Isaiah
61:1 in the synagogue (see Luke 4:18-19). He offered up His
life by the power of the Holy Spirit.

The Comforter, the Holy Spirit, has come to dwell in and with
Christians. In John 14 and 16 Jesus talks about the Holy Spirit
coming in His place to be with the disciples. They didn't fully
comprehend that after Jesus' death He would send His Spirit
to dwell in them, so He would always be with His sheep as
Shepherd and Teacher through the Holy Spirit. We see then,
when the oil is offered *with* the meal offering, this too refers
to Jesus.

Two more items were important in the meal offering—the
frankincense and salt. We'll look at the frankincense first,
then the salt.

The frankincense was an aromatic gum from a tree in the
Middle East. Gum was gathered and used in the manufacture
of incense. In Leviticus 2:2, the meal offering is said to be
a sweet savour unto the LORD. Paul verifies that Christ was
pictured in the meal offering when he says, ***And walk in love,
as Christ also hath loved us, and hath given himself for us
an offering and a sacrifice to God for a sweetsmelling
savour*** (Ephesians 5:2).

Salt was a preservative used widely in Palestine before the invention of refrigerators or other means of food preservation. The meal offering had salt added to it—no meal offering was to be without salt. Jesus' words are the salt that brings the preservation of all who hear and accept them.

Today Christians are to be salt, following in Christ's steps—we are to be heralds of God's Word and truth to a perishing world. Our walk and talk should preserve the righteousness and holiness God expects of us, His dear children. Therefore, *Let your speech be always with grace, seasoned with salt, that ye may know how ye ought to answer every man* (Colossians 4:6).

Dear Heavenly Father,

I thank You for the blood Jesus so willingly shed for me so I can approach You boldly and receive forgiveness and cleansing for my former sinful nature and for any future sins I commit. Thank You for forgiving me for all evil I have ever done.

I am so grateful to Jesus for spilling His blood for me so I am no longer separated from You. Finally, Father, I thank You for giving me peace in my mind and heart so I can rest in You in all circumstances of my life.

PRAYING THROUGH THE BRAZEN LAVER

The second piece of furniture we come to is the brazen laver. The brazen laver was used by the priests to wash themselves from the dirt of the world and the blood of the sacrifices. Brass in the Old Testament always symbolizes judgment. The brazen laver illustrates our need to be washed in the water of the Word and to apply the blood of Jesus for the cleansing of our sins on a continual basis.

BODY: God has made glorious provision for His people. Ample lessons abound throughout the pages of the Bible to show His tender care and love for humanity. Here we are introduced to a great truth through the brazen laver. It has been stated that brass is indicative of judgment; however, God's judgment always provides a clause to escape the awful consequences of disobedience.

SOUL: It is clear that God never turns a blind eye to sin. Disobedience must be expelled and punished. Through the brazen laver God has plainly depicted the means of cleansing our daily transgressions.

The cleansing God offers goes deeper than just the putting away of the filth of the flesh (see I Peter 3:21). The Word begins transforming our inclination from disobedience and rebellion against God, seeking Him to find His will for us.

SPIRIT: Early in the Biblical record, men of God knew how to receive cleansing for sins of omission or commission. Psalms 119:9,11 exquisitely and succinctly gives instruction on how to obtain cleansing for the dirt of the world that daily clings to us: *Wherewithal shall a young man cleanse his way? by taking heed thereto according to thy word. . . . Thy word have I hid in mine heart, that I might not sin against thee.*

The Apostle Peter further develops the idea that the Word washes us from daily defilement when he says:

> *Seeing ye have purified your souls in obeying the truth through the Spirit unto unfeigned love of the brethren, see that ye love one another with a pure heart fervently: Being born again, not of corruptible seed, but of incorruptible, by the word of God, which liveth and abideth for ever* (I Peter 1:22, 23).

Wonderful and marvelous is God's provision for us, allowing us to walk daily in renewed fellowship through God's cleansing agent—the Word of God. We are washed by the water of the Word and follow the standards of the Ten Commandments. Fix your eyes on Jesus, the author and finisher of our faith, having given every means to make us profitable in the Kingdom of God and to persevere unto the end.

Today, the laver represents the Word of God to us:

> *. . . Christ also loved the church, and gave himself for it; That he might sanctify and cleanse it with the washing of water by the word, That he might present it to himself a glorious church, not having spot, or wrinkle, or any such thing; but that it should be holy and without blemish* (Ephesians 5:25-27).

Let's be diligent to avail ourselves of the abundant means God gives so we may be entire, wanting nothing, knowing that it is God's good will and pleasure to give us the Kingdom (see II Peter 1:10,11; James 1:4; Luke 12:32).

Dear Heavenly Father,

Thank You for Your Word that cleanses me from the defilement of the world, refreshing me when I am weary. When tempted to sin or follow the ways of the world with all of its enticements, Your Word leads me in righteousness. As I walk through life, Your Word will be, *a lamp unto my feet, and a light unto my path* (Psalm 119:105), strengthening my walk before You, guiding my thoughts, and bringing my desires under Your control. My time will be filled with godly pursuits because I am filled with Your Word, and by daily meditating on it, I will speak words of life.

I thank You that the Word will keep my feet anchored in You.

PRAYING THROUGH THE TABLE OF SHEWBREAD

Once inside the Holy Place, the priest turns to a table, called the table of shewbread, upon which is situated twelve loaves of bread. Through the table of shewbread, God's intention is to further our understanding of the purpose of the loaves of bread. In nearly every culture, bread was a staple of life. The priest, as all people in the Semitic culture, understands that the bread sustains life and without it they would perish.

Jesus referred to Himself as the bread of life (see John 6:35). He also said He was the Living Bread that would bring eternal life to any who ate of it: *I am the living bread which came down from heaven: if any man eat of this bread, he shall live for ever . . .* (John 6:51).

BODY: Outwardly, the table of shewbread could be experienced by the senses. The loaves and table could be seen and the pure frankincense sprinkled on the loaves of bread as a memorial (see Leviticus 24:7) could be smelled. Frankincense is a costly aromatic substance with a satisfying fragrance. It was one of the gifts brought to Jesus by the Magi. Many biblical scholars believe it represents the humanity of Christ. When the priests ate the shewbread sprinkled with the frankincense, they were foreshadowing the partaking of the humanity of Christ by His Body, the Church. The priests who participated in the ceremonies lived by the offerings in the Tabernacle, including the shewbread, while humanity now lives by the offering of Christ.

SOUL: The Israelites knew God had instituted the Tabernacle ceremonies. They were able to point to the time Moses was given the directions on how to build the table of shewbread. They knew its length, breadth, and height. They could recount with certainty what materials were used in the construction of the table. Ingredients of the bread were clearly given, so the priests could make the bread. Intellectually they knew many things *about* the bread and the table, but the deeper meaning lay hidden. Jesus is the Bread of Life, the lover of our soul.

SPIRIT: Each loaf of bread on the table once consisted of individual grains of wheat. However, through the process of grinding, kneading, rising, and baking, those individual grains became molded into something useful for God's service, a means to nourish and witness to the people so they might see and discern the meaning in the loaves. The twelve loaves symbolized Israel, the people of God. Since there were twelve loaves on the table, *all* of God's people were represented, showing the completeness of God's redeemed people.

Where were the loaves of bread located? They were inside the Holy Place on the table of acacia wood overlaid with gold. The wood symbolized the humanity our Lord received from Mary, while the gold symbolized the divinity of Jesus. Mary, the handmaiden of the LORD, was overshadowed by the Holy Spirit (the same Spirit that hovered over the waters of the earth when God spoke the world into being) and was instrumental in bringing the body of the Son of God into being (see Hebrews 10:5). How does this relate to the loaves of shewbread? God invites us to partake of the Bread of Life, Jesus Christ. When we do, our humanity is transformed *and* we also partake of the divinity of Christ which becomes part of our nature as well (see II Corinthians 3:18 and II Peter 1:4).

The loaves of shewbread were replaced by the priests every Sabbath. Likewise, we cannot expect that yesterday's revelation from God's Word or that our past worship and enjoyment of Christ will sustain us in what awaits us today. Every day we need to obtain fresh nourishment from God's table of shewbread. Unless we do this we will become stale and listless in our walk with Christ. Then when we meet together for Bible study or church, we may not be in tune with the flow of the Spirit and miss something new that God wants to show us. Very few people can continually eat leftovers without becoming bored with tasting the same thing all the time. God's revelation is new all the time. His refreshing provisions flow from His throne to His children. If we are not willing to place ourselves under the blessings God has for us, then *we* will become old, stale, and listless in our Christian life. Feed on the Living Bread—taste and see that the Lord is good—Lord, give us this day, our daily bread!

Today, the Body of Christ is reflected in the loaves of bread in the Tabernacle. Paul states, *For we being many are one bread, and one body: for we are all partakers of that one bread* (I Corinthians 10:17). Once we were individual grains, but through the process of life in the Spirit, God is preparing a people that will not only refresh those around us but will also refresh God. We offer the Bread of Life, Jesus Christ, to the world as we endeavor to feed a starving and dying world. The old adage, "You are what you eat," can be applied to Christians today. By feeding on the Word of God, we will be able to offer the true, satisfying bread to give life to perishing souls.

What we feed on is what others feed on from us. We need the *rhema* of the logos. While reading the Word, have you ever noticed that a particular passage seems to be just what you need for your situation? Or perhaps you know of someone who is having a difficult time and needs a word from God, and during your meditation time, a verse from the Bible leaps out and touches your spirit, showing you this is what will meet your friend's need? This is the *rhema*, God's word to and for you! Glory be to God! Don't be satisfied with God's Word to remain only words on a page. Ask the Father, right now, to reveal Himself to you through the living, active, and powerful Word of God. It is not enough to read the words of the Bible; we must also know and experience God through the Word.

Dear Father,

You have fed me with the Living Bread, Jesus. Now show me how I may in turn offer this bread to those around me. There are many who don't know about You and are starving to know You, the True and Living God.

I consecrate my life, time, and talents to be a priest, faithful in my duties, diligent in pursuing souls for Your Kingdom. May I continually feed on the Bread of Life, fully devoted to being filled with You and to rescuing the perishing souls You bring my way. May I remember my place in the Body. Use me to feed Your people, strengthening them on their journey.

PRAYING THROUGH THE GOLDEN CANDLESTICK

We pass now from the Outer Court into the Holy Place, where the priest offers the sacrifices to make His people acceptable to God by remittance of sin through the shedding of blood and cleansing by the water in the brazen laver. Surrounded by a curtained area with no windows or discernible door, the golden candlestick illuminates the area. Beyond this obvious function of the gold lamp stand, there is a greater meaning.

The candlestick provides needed light for the priest to perform his duties in the Holy Place, alongside the table of shewbread (with the twelve loaves of bread signifying the twelve tribes of Israel) and the golden altar of incense.

BODY: God has depicted Himself as the God of light through the revelation of Scripture. Early in the Biblical record, in the first few verses of Genesis, the essence of God's being is portrayed as full of light. He cannot produce something unless it is an essential part of Who He is; man speaks out of the abundance of his heart, so God speaks out of the abundance of His heart. What is produced is a masterpiece of beauty and purpose!

Darkness is upon the face of the deep. This is apparently not acceptable to God. The Spirit of God moves upon the face of the deep, when suddenly God's voice commands, *Let there be light* and light filled the earth (Genesis 1:3). Amazingly, the God of the universe creates, in the midst of chaos and utter darkness, a foreshadowing of things that will benefit mankind for ages to come until the end of time—LIGHT! This is God's first creative act, thus a precedent is set for the future.

Throughout this survey of the furnishings of the Tabernacle, we've discovered that different articles are constructed of various materials. Here is the first mention of something made of pure gold.

The priest was responsible for keeping the reservoirs in the lamp filled with olive oil so the light would not dim or extinguish. The gold of the lamp stand, the light, the heat/flame, and the oil all indicate something other than what could be perceived by the senses.

SOUL: The Israelites knew that the items inside the Tabernacle were set apart for use by the Levites in service to God. They also knew what items were inside that part of the Tabernacle since the artisans among them were responsible for crafting those items. Materials used in the manufacture of the items were donated by the people from the spoils taken from Egypt. The Israelis' generosity was so great that they had to be restrained from giving any more for the construction of the Tabernacle. They knew only second–hand about the ministrations of the priest inside the Holy Place. Because they were thus limited to what they could observe, a gulf remained in what they knew.

SPIRIT: At the birth of Jesus Christ, God ushered in a new beginning and more details were added to the plan mapped out from the foundation of the world. God was unveiling more of who He is in the person and work of His Son.

Above, we alluded to the first creation, light. The light in the Holy Place was *adequate* for what the priest had to perform. However, more light was needed to fully reveal the mystery behind the golden lamp stand. There were certain nuances not easily discovered by the light from the candlestick.

Gold is associated with divinity in the Bible. That the material for the candlestick is gold is not incidental. What emanates from the lamp stand—light—is indicative of Jesus' divinity in His role as creator.

The Word emphasizes at that time, the appearance of Jesus Christ was *the* most important event in history. When Jesus came to earth much more light was brought into the world because the Creator of light came to dwell among men.

- His birth was preceded and accompanied by a star —Matthew 2:1-2

- His birth was prophesied to bring light—Isaiah 9:1-2, 42:5-9, Matthew 4:13-16

- He is the Light of the world—John 1:3-9; 8:12; I John 2:8

- He is the Sun of righteousness—Malachi 4:2

- He shines in our hearts—II Corinthians 4:6

What was the candlestick's purpose? It was to give light. Light is the source of sight. If there was no light in an art museum, would it matter if the most exquisite and magnificent treasures surrounded you? Groping and feeling around in the dark to examine the treasures would not allow you to experience the true beauty as would having a source of light with which to see them. However, God has not left humanity in the dark since He has caused the light of His dear Son to dispel the darkness:

> *Giving thanks unto the Father, which hath made us meet*
> *to be partakers of the inheritance of the saints in light:*
> *Who hath delivered us from the power of darkness, and*
> *hath translated us into the kingdom of his dear Son . . .*
> (Colossians 1:12-13).

Jesus Christ modeled for us what it means to live in the realm of the supernatural. His ministry came out of direct fellowship and communication with His Father. He never acted on His own, always relying upon His Father as the source of His ministry.

Likewise, as Christians, we are to live our lives and model our ministry after that of Jesus Christ. Our Savior lived constantly in the presence of God, drawing from the Father His power, inspiration, instruction, and direction. When John the Baptist was preaching repentance in Galilee, beyond the Jordan, John stated that One mightier than he was coming, One Who would baptize them in the Holy Spirit and with fire (see Matthew 3:11). The person of Whom he was speaking, of course, was Jesus.

It is not enough to have the indwelling of the Holy Spirit Who gives us light when we read and study the Word (see John 16:13; I John 2:27); we must be anointed with the fire of the Holy Spirit, fire to burn out the dross, making us as pure gold. In the process we are not merely hearing the Word, but rather, we become fountains pouring forth the Word of life into others by serving them (see James 1:22; Philippians 2:16).

Through the second birth, we bear the image of the second Adam, Jesus Christ, Who is the Light of the world. We, too, are expected to be light bearers, leading people out of the darkness into eternal light:

> *Ye are the light of the world. A city that is set on an hill cannot be hid. . . . Let your light so shine before men that they may see your good works, and glorify your Father which is in heaven* (Matthew 5:14,16).

> *Do all things without murmurings and disputings: That ye may be blameless and harmless, the sons of God, without rebuke, in the midst of a crooked and perverse nation, among whom ye shine as lights in the world . . .* (Philippians 2:14,15).

Seven branches composed the lamp stand. There was a central shaft from which six branches lifted up, three on each side of the main branch. All the branches were composed of the same material and made with the same designs (flowers and almonds) in the same way. There was uniformity and agreement in the construction of the lamp stand. All branches contained the same oil to provide the light for service in the Tabernacle.

In the Christian life, we derive our sustenance from the Vine, Jesus Christ. We are the branches. The flowers and almonds on the lamp stand indicate fruit-bearing. We are to be not only light-bearers but fruit produc-ers, too. If we are not abiding in Him, if we're cut off from the source of the Spirit (oil) that flows from Him, we will be unable to emit light or bear fruit. Our service to the Master will become worthless. There are serious conse-quences for not abiding in Him (see John 15:1-9; John 12:35-36, 44-46).

Finally, at the end of the age, God gives us a glimpse of what is to come. In Revelation, the apostle John is given a "sneak preview" of what God has in store for His loved ones. John records the vision he was given of the New Jerusalem:

> And he carried me away in the spirit to a great and
> high mountain, and shewed me that great city, the holy
> Jerusalem, descending out of heaven from God, Having
> the glory of God: and her light was like unto a stone most
> precious, even like a jasper stone, clear as crystal . . .
> And I saw no temple therein: for the Lord God Almighty
> and the Lamb are the temple of it. And the city had no
> need of the sun, neither of the moon, to shine in it: for
> the glory of God did lighten it, and the Lamb is the light
> thereof (Revelation 21:10-11, 22-23).

The Light of the world, emitting from the God of heaven will fill the city. The triumph of the Son of God will manifest completely. What began as a dim light from the golden candlestick in the Holy Place is now the glory of God and the light of the Lamb at the end of the ages.

> Now unto him that is able to keep you from falling, and
> to present you faultless before the presence of his glory
> with exceeding joy, To the only wise God our Saviour, be
> glory and majesty, dominion and power, both now and
> ever. Amen (Jude 1:24-25).

Dear Father in Heaven,

I praise You for the marvelous things I behold out of Your law. Thank You for illuminating my eyes, for giving me wisdom, and for giving me the insight of the Holy Spirit.

You are my teacher. May I always hear Your voice and continually abide in Christ as a light to those around me. Let me bear much fruit so You, Father, are glorified in my life.

I thank You that the Spirit of the Lord rests upon me, the Spirit of wisdom and understanding are upon me Lord. Make me wise in ways to serve You. Fill me with understanding and give me the mind of the Lord.

I believe You for the Spirit of counsel and might, so I know the right thing to do and the right word to say in every situation. Because I have the Spirit of might, I can bring down every stronghold of the enemy and defeat him that comes to kill, steal, and destroy.

You give me the Spirit of knowledge that leads me into all truth and fills me with all the knowledge of the Lord.

I have the fear of the Lord, knowing that is the beginning of knowledge. I do not fear what man can do to me, *For God hath not given us the spirit of fear; but of power, and of love, and of a sound mind* (2 Timothy 1:7).

Today I live for YOU knowing I'm empowered to walk in victory!

PRAYING THROUGH THE ALTAR OF INCENSE

The priest has gone past the table of shewbread and the golden candlestick. He has been reminded that the twelve tribes of Israel are represented as God's united people by the loaves of bread. Because of the light provided by the golden candlestick, he has been enabled to see the deep mysteries of God for the chosen nation—they are to be witnesses, a light, to lead the nations around them into the true worship of the living God. Now, the priest is ready to offer up prayer for the needs of the Israelites, assured his ministrations have been accepted by God because he has performed them in the way the Lord commanded Moses. Perhaps now, the priest will conduct one of the most important parts of his ministry, prayer.

BODY: Prayer is not a matter of the position of the body but an attitude of the heart. People in the Bible prayed standing, kneeling, or lying prostrate on the ground. There is no prescribed "correct" way to pray. Kneeling is not any more effective than standing. Whether you pray with your eyes open or closed, with your hands outstretched or folded—prayer presents to God the needs that burden us and our loved ones.

> *Be careful for nothing; but in every thing by prayer*
> *and supplication with thanksgiving let your requests*
> *be made known unto God. And the peace of God,*
> *which passeth all understanding, shall keep your hearts*
> *and minds through Christ Jesus* (Philippians 4:6-7).

SOUL: We can approach prayer as work or a duty, or we can view it as a blessed and creative event—our heavenly Father is inviting us into His presence so He can spend time with His loved ones. He is the great ruler and authority of the universe, yet we call Him Abba Father (Daddy). We bring with us into the throne room, our petitions, concerns, needs, and desires. The priests of the Tabernacle were commissioned to intercede for Israel. Today, *every* believer can come into the holy place to seek the face of God.

According to Revelation 8, incense is mixed with the prayers of the saints as they ascend to God. Every prayer is attentively heard by our great High Priest, Jesus. He is at the right hand of the Father eagerly anticipating our requests. Our Lord wants to grant every petition that reaches His ears. Why? He loves us more than a father loves his son. God will give us what will gladden our hearts and make our joy complete (see Matthew 7:7-12; John 16:23-27). One thing we must remember as we pray—our aim and goal should be to touch God in the realm of the Spirit.

SPIRIT: God's wisdom and intentions for His children flow from His Word. The Apostle Paul explains to the church at Corinth, *I will pray with the spirit, and I will pray with the understanding also . . .* (I Corinthians 14:15). God has given us the gift of praying in the Spirit. There may be times when human words fail us. We may not know what to pray for, but the Spirit of Him who raised Jesus from the dead dwells in us interceding for us in those times of unknowing and uncertainty:

> *Likewise the Spirit also helpeth our infirmities: for we know not what we should pray for as we ought: but the Spirit itself maketh intercession for us with groanings which cannot be uttered. And he that searcheth the hearts knoweth what is the mind of the Spirit, because he maketh intercession for the saints according to the will of God* (Romans 8:26-27).

Approaching God by praying in the Spirit will help take our minds off the problems and challenges facing us and to fully enter the presence of God. When you pray, focus on the Giver of all good things not the things themselves. Our motives and ideas must come into compliance with God's will. His will for us is that we might be filled with joy and that all of our needs might be fulfilled. We may not be aware that sometimes our desires, even though good, may not match God's highest good for us. That is why prayer in the Spirit is of utmost importance to the believer!

There is much in the pages of the Word that apply to prayer. Let's touch briefly on some of the highlights.

- Pray in the Spirit—I Corinthians 14:15; Ephesians 6:18

- Pray without ceasing—I Thessalonians 5:17

- Pray for everything—Philippians 4:6

- Pray for all men everywhere—I Timothy 2:1-3, 8

- Pray for the household of faith—I Thessalonians 5:25; II Thessalonians 1:11

- Pray for the sick—James 5:13-16

Today, as believers, we are privileged to enter into the ministry of prayer not only for ourselves and our needs, but we are blessed to be able to intercede on behalf of people in need around us. Friends, loved ones, neighbors, co-workers may have only one person to pray for them—you. Your intercession may be the only thing standing between them and an excruciating eternity separated from God. Your one prayer may be what brings them the assurance of eternal life with God in heaven. Your prayer may usher them into a life of blessing and release from a curse. May your prayer be that of the psalmist, *Let my prayer be set forth before thee as incense . . .* (Psalm 141:2).

As the altar of incense is examined, you may be encouraged to enter more often and fully into the ministry of prayer. You will not only reap the benefits by praying, but you will be the source of blessing to others, as you stand before God's throne offering the incense of prayer to your heavenly Father.

We've all heard practice makes perfect. Do not neglect practicing and entering the ministry of prayer with faith and anticipation. So much and so many are depending on your faithful intercession for them. We are priests of prayer, called by our faithful God and our High Priest, Jesus, to send the sweet fragrance of incense—prayer—into the throne room of grace. God awaits! Don't delay! Enter His presence today!

Dear Heavenly Father,

I thank You that because of Jesus, I am free to come boldly into Your presence. Through Jesus, You have made me righteous and sanctified so I may draw near to You.

Father, I ask You to teach me to pray more accurately with the direction of the Holy Spirit and the guidance of the Word of God. Help me to pray Your will, regardless of the state of my emotions. Most of all, I ask You to teach me how to commune with You in deeper, more intimate ways. I love You, Father, and want to know You more fully each and every day.

PRAYING THROUGH THE ARK OF THE COVENANT

As he does once a year, the high priest enters into the Holy of Holies to offer the blood of a sacrificial animal for the cleansing and remission of the sins of Israel. No one except God's chosen representative from among the Levitical priesthood can enter this sacred place. Before he enters there to meet with God for the Chosen Nation, the priest must be cleansed with blood from any sins that he may have committed during the previous year.

BODY: When he entered the Holy of Holies what would the priest find? Before him, he would see a box of wood overlaid with gold. Inside the Ark were tokens of God's presence and care of Israel—the golden pot of manna, Aaron's budded rod, and the tablets containing the Law written by the finger of God (see Hebrews 9:4) and the books of the Pentateuch.

Each item placed in the Ark had the definite imprint of God's intervention for Israel. Why were these particular items placed in the Ark of the Covenant? A marvelous mystery unfolds when we examine these items. God has lessons for Christians today that can be learned from the Ark and its contents, the depths of which were only remotely understood or discerned by the people of Israel.

SOUL: If we could have interviewed the Hebrews after they had been recently rescued from slavery in Egypt and asked them, "What is the meaning of the manna, Aaron's rod, and the stone tablets?" it is doubtful they would have been able to give more than a simple answer.

They certainly could recount the sudden appearance of manna from the sky, Moses' trek up the mountain, shrouded in forty days of mystery until he descended with the laws of God, and the rod of Aaron that suddenly blossomed. They knew the solid, material signs and symbols of the items in the Ark and their experience but not the reality of them.

SPIRIT: The Ark itself was not particularly stunning or outstanding in its appearance. It was constructed of shittim wood, which Bible scholars believe was acacia, the most indestructible wood available. Though overlaid with gold, one would not be especially drawn to its outward beauty. However, God's lesson in the Ark lay in the materials used in its construction. The wood was a product of the earth that had grown in the hard environment of the desert. Just as the first Adam was born of the earth, his body formed of earthly elements, so the Last Adam, Jesus, shared in the same humanity, subject to the same limitations as all of mankind.

Yet, He shared another characteristic not common to humans—He was God's *only* Son, conceived by the Holy Spirit, born of a virgin (see Isaiah 7:14; 9:6-7).

> *In the beginning was the Word, and the Word was with God, and the Word was God* (John 1:1).

> *And the Word was made flesh, and dwelt among us, (and we beheld his glory, the glory as of the only begotten of the Father,) full of grace and truth* (John 1:14).

Thus, the gold indicates the divinity of Jesus Christ. The Israelites carried the Ark of the Covenant into battle. As long as they had the Ark and followed God's directives, the Israelites knew they would win any battle they fought. Jesus is our Ark of the Covenant. With Him as our Commander, we know we will prevail over every foe and emerge safe and victorious. *Nay, in all these things we are more than conquerors through him that loved us* (Romans 8:37).

Aaron's rod that budded was not merely a creative miracle to prove to the people that Aaron was chosen as God's authoritative spokesman. In addition to the obvious there was a veiled reference to Jesus. There are several passages in the Old and New Testaments indicating that the rod actually refers to Jesus:

> *And there shall come forth a rod out of the stem of Jesse, and a Branch shall grow out of his roots: And the spirit of the LORD shall rest upon him, the spirit of wisdom and understanding, the spirit of counsel and might, the spirit of knowledge and of the fear of the LORD . . .* (Isaiah 11:1-2).

Behold, the days come, saith the LORD, that I will raise unto David a righteous Branch, and a King shall reign and prosper, and shall execute judgment and justice in the earth (Jeremiah 23:5).

And one of the elders saith unto me, Weep not: behold, the Lion of the tribe of Judah, the Root of David, hath prevailed to open the book . . . (Revelation 5:5).

When Jesus came, God's plans were fulfilled in Him (see Galatians 4:4-5). The budding rod of Aaron is a picture of the resurrection life. There was *no* life in the rod Aaron carried with him from Egypt into the wilderness, it was simply a dead stick. However, in order to prove to the Israelites that God was the God of resurrection, He caused the rod to blossom. Jesus derived life from His close fellowship with the Father, yes, but He has, residing in Himself, the nature of divinity, *For in him dwelleth all the fullness of the Godhead bodily* (Colossians 2:9).

Only God can bring to life something that is dead, as Jesus stated:

. . . I lay down my life, that I might take it again. No man taketh it from me, but I lay it down of myself. I have power to lay it down, and I have power to take it again. This commandment have I received of my Father (John 10:17-18).

Jesus has prevailed over death, hell, and the grave! Therefore, with Paul, we can boldly proclaim:

O death, where is thy sting? O grave, where is thy victory? The sting of death is sin; and the strength of sin is the law. But thanks be to God, which giveth us the victory through our Lord Jesus Christ (I Corinthians 15:55-57).

What a wonderful salvation and Savior!

Next we will examine the significance of the golden pot and the manna. As stated elsewhere, gold is a symbol of divinity. Until the New Testament was written, the revelation that the manna was in a golden pot wasn't known. However, the author of Hebrews sheds more light on this aspect of the Tabernacle furnishings:

For there was a tabernacle made . . . Which had the golden censer, and the ark of the covenant overlaid round about

with gold, wherein was the golden pot that had manna . . .
(Hebrews 9:2,4).

BODY: Gold has been considered by many societies to be a precious commodity. But Jesus said:

> *Lay not up for yourselves treasures upon earth, where*
> *moth and rust doth corrupt, and where thieves break*
> *through and steal: But lay up for yourselves treasures*
> *in heaven, where neither moth nor rust doth corrupt,*
> *and where thieves do not break through nor steal:*
> *For where your treasure is, there will your heart be also*
> *(Matthew 6:19-21).*

Further on, in Matthew 6, the people listening to Jesus' message were told not to worry about food, clothing, or other things, for they had no control over such things, and could only trust God for their provisions. All too often men seek after things that cannot satisfy, settling for substitutes without eternal value.

SOUL: What motivates people to seek after things that don't satisfy the deep longings of their souls? People try prestige, power, position, or wealth—but inwardly there may be no real joy, peace, or happiness. There is no substitute for what God offers us in Jesus Christ.

SPIRIT: Peter reminds the Christians under his care in I Peter 1:18-19:

> *Forasmuch as ye know that ye were not redeemed with*
> *corruptible things, as silver and gold . . . But with the*
> *precious blood of Christ, as of a lamb without blemish*
> *and without spot . . .*

God wanted to fill and infuse mankind with His own life in order to be reflected through humanity to principalities, powers, and the devil, both now and in the ages to come.

> *And to you who are troubled rest with us, when the*
> *Lord Jesus shall be revealed from heaven with his mighty*
> *angels, In flaming fire taking vengeance on them that know*
> *not God, and that obey not the gospel of our Lord Jesus*
> *Christ: Who shall be punished with everlasting destruction*
> *from the presence of the Lord, and from the glory of his*
> *power; When he shall come to be glorified in his saints,*

and to be admired in all them that believe (because our testimony among you was believed) in that day (II Thessalonians 1:7-10).

Paul further develops this thought in Romans 8:19, *For the earnest expectation of the creature waiteth for the manifestation of the sons of God.* As Christians who share the life of God with Christ our brother (see Hebrews 2:11), we are being transformed to reflect the nature of God.

Inside the golden pot there was a remnant of the manna God fed the children of Israel in the wilderness. Jesus told a crowd one day:

Labour not for the meat which perisheth, but for that meat which endureth unto everlasting life, which the Son of man shall give unto you: for him hath God the Father sealed (John 6:27).

Then this exchange took place between Jesus and the crowd:

Our fathers did eat manna in the desert; as it is written, He gave them bread from heaven to eat. Then Jesus said unto them, Verily, verily, I say unto you, Moses gave you not that bread from heaven; but my Father giveth you the true bread from heaven. For the bread of God is he which cometh down from heaven, and giveth life unto the world (John 6:31-33).

Jesus is the **real** manna that gives eternal life to all those who believe, trust, and act on the words of Jesus.

I am the living bread which came down from heaven: if any man eat of this bread, he shall live for ever: and the bread that I will give is my flesh, which I will give for the life of the world (John 6:51).

Lastly, we find in the Ark of the Covenant the tablets containing the Law God gave to Moses on the mount. If the Hebrews obeyed those laws, God guaranteed victory in every military campaign, possession of all land where they placed their foot, and prosperity beyond their imagination. What then was the outcome of so simple a request from the mouth of God?

BODY: It is important to remember God loves us very much. He only wants to give us the best that He has. How amazed the Israelites must have been when Moses recounted the events on the mountain: God's appearance in the cloud, God's voice speaking directly to Him about the future of the nation of Israel, and God's finger engraving the Law on two tablets of stone.

SOUL: The children of Israel accepted with awe the message from God via Moses. There was only one glitch—the people thought they could perform the Law by sheer will power. What they did not know and may not have been able to know was that they could not outwardly keep the Law perfectly. It was impossible to keep the Law because it was not given to be kept but to point the only way to eternal life through Jesus Christ.

SPIRIT: Only one person has ever fulfilled the whole Law. All others were incapable of carrying out the dictates of the Law. In fact, the Law was given to condemn us and to show haughty, proud, self-centered man his inability to be accepted by God through works. But thanks be to God that He has made The Way for us to be free from the curse and bondage of the law so we might live in power unto God (see Matthew 5:17; Romans 7:7,24-25; Galatians 3:23-26).

God didn't intend for the Law to remain on the tablet of stones as a testimony to the world of His existence, righteousness, justice, and love. In Ezekiel 36:24-27 the Lord spoke to the prophet bidding him to record for posterity the following words and prediction:

> *For I will take you from among the heathen, and gather you out of all countries, and will bring you into your own land. Then will I sprinkle clean water upon you, and ye shall be clean: from all your filthiness, and from all your idols, will I cleanse you. A new heart also will I give you, and a new spirit will I put within you: and I will take away the stony heart out of your flesh, and I will give you an heart of flesh. And I will put my spirit within you, and cause you to walk in my statutes, and ye shall keep my judgments, and do them.*

Jeremiah confirms the change from an outward performance of duty to an inward observance of God's laws and ordinances:

> *But this shall be the covenant that I will make with the house of Israel; After those days, saith the LORD, I will put my law in their inward parts, and write it in their hearts; and will be their God, and they shall be my people* (Jeremiah 31:33).

Thus, we see the magnificence of God's provision mirrored in the items in the Ark of the Covenant. Can we do anything else but praise our mighty, awesome God for all He has done for His people? As we pause on the verge of viewing the mercy seat and what God wishes for us to learn through it, let's offer this praise penned by Paul found in I Timothy 1:17: *Now unto the King eternal, immortal, invisible, the only wise God, be honour and glory for ever and ever. Amen.*

Dear Father,

I am so grateful to You for being my Provider. You abundantly meet my every need. You won't allow the righteous to go hungry, and You satisfy those who trust You. In Jesus' name, I have shelter, clothing, health, and financial help. I refuse to let anyone but You be my source of supply.

Father, in Your Son Jesus Christ is resurrection life. You have given me this new life so I can walk free from sin, successfully resisting temptation in all my ways as I yield to Your way. Jesus, You are the Vine, and as one of Your branches, I rejoice that I can and do, bear godly fruit.

Father, in Jesus, I've been made *more than* a conqueror—all the works and plans of the evil one are defeated through your power. Jesus, You are my Commander-in-Chief, I submit to Your leading, and because of You, I continually triumph over any enemy that confronts me. Thank You, Abba Father, for Your divine protection. I trust in the shelter of Your wings. With great expectation, I wait for your coming so the work you've begun in me will be completed! Even so, come Lord Jesus.

PRAYING THROUGH THE MERCY SEAT

Standing before the mercy seat, the high priest gazes on the two golden cherubim, which stood as mute witnesses to the meeting place of God with man. The priest prepares himself to offer the blood of the sacrifice to satisfy God's justice for one more year. Here in the Holy of Holies God speaks to the high priest, assuring him and the people their offering has been accepted and their sins forgiven for another year.

BODY: The bells on the priest's robe could be heard inside the Holy of Holies as he ministered for the people before the Lord. Every swish could be heard as he sprinkled blood first on the mercy seat and then seven more times in front of it. Would their sacrifice be accepted by God? Would the justice of God be satisfied yet again? Or had someone done something so wicked that God would demand punishment, making the sacrifice null and void? The people had to wait and see if the blood pleased the Lord, if they could hear the jingle of the bells on the bottom of the high priest's robe, then they knew God was not displeased with them and the sacrifice had been accepted. The rope attached to his ankle would be unnecessary. The priest was alive and could leave the Holy of Holies on his own power; however, if all had not gone well, they would have used the rope to pull the body of the priest out of the Holy of Holies.

SOUL: What did the Israelites truly know of what went on inside the Holy of Holies as the priest ministered? No one but the high priest was allowed inside that area of the Tabernacle. All entrance beyond the thick veil was forbidden to any other priest or to the common people—any who dared defy that command would be struck dead by God's power. Fear was pervasive and could be felt. Each time the priest entered the Holy of Holies questions would arise: Would the sacrifice be accepted? Would the high priest be struck dead for sins he had committed or on account of the sins of the people? The ritual progressed year after year, sacrifice after sacrifice, but the knowledge of what occurred remained rooted in the past, clouded by an uncertain future, blinded by a hardness of heart.

SPIRIT: In ages past, among the dunes and desert wastes of Sinai, God's intention for His people and the inhabitants of earth was unfolding, waiting to climax into the greatest event in the history of mankind. Planned from the foundation of the world, God's ultimate mystery would appear in the person of Jesus Christ.

> *Mercy and truth are met together; righteousness and peace have kissed each other. Truth shall spring out of the earth; and righteousness shall look down from heaven. Yea, the LORD shall give that which is good; and our land shall yield her increase. Righteousness shall go before him; and shall set us in the way of his steps* (Psalms 85:10-13).

God's desire was to meet with His people and offer them mercy at the mercy seat. Since God is infinitely holy, with no sin, He cannot accept anything stained or tainted with sin. He made provision to extend full fellowship with Israel through the sprinkled blood and the mercy seat.

Yet, there was still a barrier between *all* the people and God. God desired more than just the high priest to meet with Him once a year and have him tell the people that their sins were forgiven. God's plan was that every person who wanted could have a relationship with Him. Instead of a distant and impersonal relationship, God wanted to commune with mankind face-to-face.

The exalted, sovereign Creator of the universe therefore humbled Himself and took the form of a servant so He could walk among men, be subject to the same temptations, trials, and tribulations. Jesus was God's answer to the dilemma of separation between God and men.

John, the apostle sums up in two short verses the end result of eons of planning by God: *For the law was given by Moses, but grace and truth came by Jesus Christ. No man hath seen God at any time, the only begotten Son, which is in the bosom of the Father, he hath declared him* (John 1:17-18).

Completely unable to keep the demands of the law, let alone fulfill even the smallest command of the law, man finds himself wooed by the Son of God Who brings grace to the human race. Once the law had been given, men understood the penalty of every violation. By breaking one of the laws of God, one became guilty of breaking all the laws. The penalty was death, but through Jesus, men were to receive from the hand of God mercy, grace, and life instead of judgment and condemnation.

The picture of mercy depicted in the mercy seat finally became a reality in the person and work of Jesus Christ. He is our High Priest Who has satisfied the righteous demands of the law, as it says in Ezekiel 18:4, *. . . the soul that sinneth, it shall die.* Also, Paul declares, *For the wages of sin is death; but the gift of God is eternal life through Jesus Christ our Lord* (Romans 6:23). Throughout His earthly ministry, mercy pervaded all Jesus said and did. When He exposed the sin of the woman at the well, He offered forgiveness. He spared a woman from being stoned for adultery, then He forgave her. Even a gentile who had no place in the covenant relationship between God and Israel received healing for her sick daughter from the gracious hand of the Savior.

On the day of the crucifixion, the finality of God's eternal intentions for the human race was realized. When Jesus uttered the words, "It is finished!" and the veil between the Holy of Holies was torn in two—the desire of God came to fruition. Unobstructed fellowship was now possible through the perfect sacrifice of the Lamb of God. Hallelujah!

Having therefore, brethren, boldness to enter into the holiest by the blood of Jesus, By a new and living way, which he hath consecrated for us, through the veil,

that is to say, his flesh; And having an high priest over
the house of God . . . (Hebrews 10:19-21).

Now, man can approach God as a child approaches his father, not fearing anger or retribution. God has established His righteous kingdom. Once hidden in ages past, it is now made manifest in these last days:

Even the mystery which hath been hid from ages and
from generations, but now is made manifest to his saints:
To whom God would make known what is the riches of
the glory of this mystery among the Gentiles; which is
Christ in you, the hope of glory . . . (Colossians 1:26-27).

Closing with this passage from Hebrews will hopefully help you to grasp with assurance the completeness and trustworthiness of God's plan.

For when Moses had spoken every precept to all
the people according to the law, he took the blood of
calves and of goats, with water, and scarlet wool, and
hyssop, and sprinkled both the book, and all the people,
Saying, This is the blood of the testament which God
hath enjoined unto you. Moreover he sprinkled with
blood both the tabernacle, and all the vessels of
the ministry. And almost all things are by the law
purged with blood; and without shedding of blood
is no remission. It was therefore necessary that the
patterns of things in the heavens should be purified
with these; but the heavenly things themselves with
better sacrifices than these. For Christ is not entered
into the holy places made with hands, which are the
figures of the true; but into heaven itself, now to
appear in the presence of God for us: Nor yet that
he should offer himself often, as the high priest
entereth into the holy place every year with blood
of others; For then must he often have suffered since
the foundation of the world: but now once in the end
of the world hath he appeared to put away sin by the
sacrifice of himself. And as it is appointed unto men
once to die, but after this the judgment: So Christ
was once offered to bear the sins of many; and unto
them that look for him shall he appear the second
time without sin unto salvation (Hebrews 9:19-28).

Dear Heavenly Father,

Your Son Jesus has opened the way into the Holy of Holies, so I can commune with You, with nothing separating us.

Jesus shed His blood so I can come continually to find forgiveness of sins. His blood is sprinkled on the mercy seat in the heavenly Tabernacle as a testimony to His perfect work of redemption. He made one sacrifice, once and for all, that satisfied the Father's heart. God is well pleased with His Son.

Since I have trusted and believed in the finished work of Christ on the cross, in the words of the old *Rock of Ages* hymn, "Nothing in my hand I bring, simply to the Cross I cling," I come boldly into the presence, the Shekinah glory, of the coming King. I am accepted as beloved; nothing can separate me from the love of God.

I proclaim that I have all the privileges and rights of a child of God. With Christ, I am an heir of God! I begin to walk in that assurance.

Notes

Notes

Notes

_____

_____

_____

_____

_____

_____

_____

_____

_____

_____

_____

_____

_____

_____

Bibliography

Gaglardi, B. Maureen. *The Path of the Just. Vol. 1,* Vancouver: New West Press, 1963.

Laney, Jewell. *The Tabernacle In The Wilderness.* Columbus, GA: Brentwood Christian Press, 1989.

Pink, Arthur W. *Gleanings in Exodus.* Chicago: Moody Press, 1981.

Slemming, C. W. *Made According To Pattern.* First American edition, Fort Washington, PA: Christian Literature Crusade, 1971.